Europe
at the
Crossroads

Europe
at the
Crossroads

**A Reporter
Looks at Europe's
Spiritual Crisis**

by Wallace Henley

GOOD NEWS PUBLISHERS
Westchester, Illinois 60153

EUROPE AT THE CROSSROADS
A Reporter Looks at Europe's Spiritual Crisis

Copyright © 1978 by Good News Publishers
Westchester, Illinois 60153
All rights reserved.
Printed in the United States of America.

Library of Congress Catalog Card Number 78-68409
ISBN 0-89107-156-3

Contents

Contents

Preface

For many Americans Europe, the land of their ancestors, holds a curious mystique. I confess I have not been immune to this attraction. But four trips to Europe had only sparked the questions. I wanted to know more, and that seemed like a sufficient reason for writing a book.

So often, I knew, trends were born in Europe and in their adolescence leaped the Atlantic, to mature in America. I wanted to know what would happen to us next. But I wanted to know because I count French Huguenots among my ancestors, as well as English Anglicans. I wanted to know because I have heritage from the Anabaptists and from John Calvin and from Martin Luther and, yes, from Augustine.

I wanted to know about this place called Europe. I wanted to know why on the one hand she could give birth to a child like Wagner, composing his arrogant, brash music, and also bring forth a Bach, carefully copying music in his tyrannical brother's library so he could compose works to glorify God.

7

I wanted to know about this land that gave us Hitler in his mad ragings and Helmut Thielicke and Martin Niemöller courageously persevering in their bombed-out pulpits.

I wanted to know about this place where Paul Tournier has recorded his sublime understandings of human nature, as seen through the Bible, yet where Freud had reduced man to a creature in bondage to subconscious sexual forces.

I wanted to know about Europe, a land where Nietszche pioneered the idea of the death of God in the nineteenth century, but also a land which, in a later time, nurtured the growth of a C. S. Lewis and a J. R. R. Tolkien and their beautiful parables of the Kingdom.

I wanted to know the part of the world where medieval artisans raised stone symphonies to the glory of God and where, centuries later, 20th-century technocrats would build squat gas furnaces to the glory of Satan.

So I went back again, asking questions. I did not learn everything. But I learned enough to believe that Europe is at the most crucial period of its history since the Reformation.

Wallace Henley
September, 1977

Introduction

Europe appears to be a continent on the verge of moral collapse. Decades of anemic Christianity and humanistic philosophies have eaten the spiritual interior of this continent and Europe now stands at a crossroads. Can it be saved?

How has this all come about? North American audiences will richly profit from a study of this book by Wallace Henley. Americans may be encouraged by their own spiritual heritage and they may be warned by European trends recognizable within our own country and churches. Many tourists, students, and even missionaries stand in awe of the European mind and theologians. Indirectly Henley reminds us that we need not have an inferiority complex, but that a simple Gospel message, deep commitment to Jesus Christ and a life pleasing to God is, indeed, the spiritual dynamic that has been "salt" in our society.

On a number of occasions evangelical theologians and even mission administrators have deplored the "naive" evangelicalism of the United States. With all

our faults and failures, this has *not* been one of them.
After over 20 years of evangelism and theological training in Europe it was difficult to see any positive or
constructive influence of the great European theologians upon the growth of secularism in Europe. Yet
American pastors and professors often quote them
profusely with awe. There seems to be little evangelism, church planting or church growth resulting from
their prodigious labors.

Europe is characterized by the state church concept which had its roots in Constantine and the fourth
century A.D. Every state church has its parish or
geographical area of influence. When we began to
"plant" a church in the southern suburbs of Paris, for
example, the Protestant pastor could not accept the
idea that this was not to be a new effort contributing
to his own parish work. We saw it from the "free
church" concept of the United States where church
membership is *voluntary* and where we may attend
the church of our choice in a religiously *pluralistic*
society. One is not born a Christian, but one becomes
a Christian by personal faith and trust in Jesus Christ
as Savior and Lord. Now, however, in the strong
secularization of European society the state church
system is in trouble because fewer and fewer are willing to make a payroll deduction that will go to support
the state church.

But it is not the state church system itself that has
brought the present spiritual drought in both Roman
Catholicism and Protestantism in Europe. The
century-long erosion of biblical authority has done
this. Pastors and even evangelists cannot say "God

10

says," "The Bible says," or "Thus saith the Lord" because they are not sure that what the Bible says is true. The verbal inerrancy and infallibility of the Bible has been questioned by seminary theologians and pastors for over a century. Consequently, there is no more word from God and many are looking to the authority of the Church as Tradition, to God as he speaks in world events, or to a mystical experience of some kind divorced from biblical norms.

A new understanding of culture has also contributed to this confusion. If the Old Testament was written in a Jewish culture and the New Testament was influenced by Greek culture how can we, they say, understand and apply the Bible today in our modern technological society. So the European theologian often looks for "God's word" in the Bible as God speaks to him. Truth, they say, is not propositional and, therefore, we cannot take doctrinal statements literally, for those of the early Church councils or the Reformation of the 16th century were in another culture. We must get to the "matter," the kernel of truth and not be concerned about the "form," the words and culture in which it was written. It is of great importance to a ministry in Europe to remember that God has given us a "body of truth" inerrantly inspired by the Holy Spirit and that this "corpus of truth" is unchangeable, yet applicable to all cultures and continents. A study of the behavioral sciences and the philosophy of communication should not lead us to complicate and confuse our interpretation of the Scripture. The Holy Spirit who inspired the Scripture also is constantly "in, with and by the Scripture." He applies the Scripture to the need of every culture in every era of history. Our business is to "preach the Word" in Europe. Those who have done so have found that it works.

The result of this confusion in biblical interpretation has produced a theological pluralism and relativism. That is, some would say, you evangelicals have your way of interpreting the Bible literally and other continents and cultures have theirs. Evangelical belief in the necessity of the "new birth" is not necessarily applicable to the Eastern Orthodox churches, or to the Roman Catholic Church of Western Europe, to Africa, etc. The result is evident in the World Council of Churches with headquarters in Geneva: all churches are right in their own way. If we cannot fully depend upon the Bible to be the norm of truth we can, at least, depend upon the "tradition" of the Church in history. Many today are unaware that European Protestantism is without a theological anchor and is moving year by year toward union with Roman Catholicism, a union based on the Tradition of the Church and the Bible as part of its tradition. This is a return to a pre-Reformation position. The great questions today are:

1. What is a Christian?
2. What is a Christian church?
3. How can we know what God's final authority to man is?

Another current in Europe is the emphasis upon restructuring society. The evangelicals, traditional religion declares, are pietists who withdraw from the needs of society and are only concerned with the "souls" of men. Responsible Christianity, they say, must recognize that Christ not only died for all men (universalism in one form or another) but that Christ is LORD of all the creation into which he was born and for which he died. Since society *is* redeemed now, it is the responsibility of the Christians to occupy and possess *now* that over which Christ *is now* Lord. For them there is no personal Satan—only the demonic powers associated most frequently with capitalistic oppressors. The ideal and Christian political system is a socialism toward which Christians are to work. "Evangelism" and "salvation" are associated by European theologians and the WCC with the introduction of a "just society" which is man's salvation—a temporal salvation.

What is the answer to Europe's spiritual needs? While all is in the hands of a sovereign God, it would seem that the best answer lies in an abundant evangelical evangelism, church planting and church growth. It seems humanly impossible and even wishful thinking to suppose that para-church organizations can "infiltrate" the entire established religions and theological system of Europe and, thereby, renew their spiritual life. God by his servants within these institutional churches can if he wills, but this does not seem to be the role of the missionaries coming from across the seas. Evangelism and church planting has been a slow but fruitful process in several places in Europe. These evangelical churches have spiritual life in Christ and are multiplying.

It is the *message* more than the *method* that is deficient in Western Europe. For some, even in

13

evangelical ranks, there is no eternal punishment, no hell, for God is too good to so condemn people. This universalism has cut the vital cords of man's need. The Gospel becomes an addition to the "good life" or a way to it. The Gospel is something man can live with or live without. If he does not have it now, it is said, God will in love provide it in eternity.

God is working through European evangelicals and there are leaders of great spiritual and intellectual stature. Yet it is evident that Europe is a mission field in need of missionaries with good theologies, clear ecclesiologies and warm hearts. Evangelization in Europe begins with a good message, for good theology will result in great doxology. "It is difficult to be continually enthusiastic about nothing!"

Arthur P. Johnston, Ph.D.
Professor of Missions and
Director of the Program
of World Evangelism
Trinity Evangelical Divinity School

CHAPTER ONE

Faces of Europe

The train squeals through Neuchatel. Over the seat facing me, Brezhnev waves a greeting. Brezhnev is a teddy bear, held by a happy Dutch lady going home from a Swiss holiday. The slender woman is perhaps 50. Her teenage daughter sits beside her, a little embarrassed at her mother's waving the bear's hand and telling the American passenger that she has decided to call the furry thing Brezhnev. We laugh. There is a cry for help rumbling somewhere beneath the lilt of the giggle.

The five Dutch sitting in the double chairs which face each other invite us to join them. A tall, pleasant woman quietly explains to me the purpose of their trip. She is the hostess for the small band. They are Dutch Resistance veterans. Their nerves are still seared from the terror of 30 years ago. A wealthy Dutchman provides them a periodic vacation to Switzerland to help them forget—"the healing of memories," an acquaintance of mine once put it. The lady clutching Brezhnev has much to forget—like hurling Molotov cocktails at Nazis. Across from her is another woman, trying to forget the bullet which split her skull. Her husband, a friendly cheesemaker, holds her hand and smiles. They have forgotten enough for awhile. Home will look good again.

The train rolls on toward Basel. It is nearly 11 P.M. We have all been up a long time, and soon are awash in the giddiness that comes with weariness. We laugh and sing. There's no one else in the car—just the Dutch and we two Americans trying to probe Europe's spiritual tone.

But now the mood shifts. Yes, they've heard of Corrie ten Boom. Tante Corrie, so far away, is the door through which we offer a witness about Jesus. My friend talks; I pray. After awhile, Brezhnev's master indicates a deeper response to this talk about Jesus. Her teenage daughter is listening, too. They take booklets describing the joy of walking in the Holy Spirit. The tall lady who is the hostess is weeping quietly. "That is what she needs," she repeats. She embraces my friend, who's been doing the witnessing. She gives me her name and address in Amsterdam. Whenever I am in Holland, I am part of her family; I have a home. We shared Christ with her tortured friend.

My assumptions about the impenetrable Europeans are shaken.

* * *

Jose Montanes is as much the embodiment of Spain as Charles de Gaulle was France. One suspects he suppresses the urge to break out into a Flamenco dance.

We meet at a conference in northern Europe. Jose is an affluent businessman in Barcelona. But he moves around Europe, encouraging small groups of believers and nonbelievers to come together for talk that always winds up on the theme of Christ as the solution to Europe's crisis.

Twenty of them sit around the table as Jose speaks. They are from Belgium, England, West Germany, the Netherlands, Turkey. French gives way to English. Their languages are different. But they are of the same family: followers of Christ.

The conversations begin.

"God cares about persons, not about kingdoms," observes a participant, a bank executive from France.

"The personal relationship with Christ is critical," responds a British television executive. "This relationship through the ages has produced principles; but they are not as important as the relationship."

The discussions weave into the dark tapestry of the night until the participants adjourn to tiny rooms where they will rest before resuming the talks in the morning.

As the year moves along, there will be many more such talks all over Europe about the relevancy of Jesus Christ. Some of the nonbelievers will scarcely believe they're participating in such talk. But they will be present because Jose Montanes invited them. In a society greatly impressed by aristocracy and sophistication, Jose's influence weighs a ton.

* * *

Monsieur Jean Rey was for six years president of the European Economic Community. But there is another community which gets much of his interest—the community of believers in Christ.

When Montanes and his companions get together, Jean Rey is likely to be there. He is a politician who speaks with the compassion of a pastor, the depth of a scholar and the wit of a refined comedian. There is a kind of transcendent cast about the man. Heaven and earth touch in him, and the places on earth he touches are better because heaven touches him.

Once, asked to sum up a weekend of "conversations" about Christ and public issues, Jean Rey said: "We are just as confused as we were when we began, except now we are confused on a deeper level."

* * *

"Catalyst" is the title one might hang on Wallace Haines. Home is a neat cottage tucked into a glade near Ascot, England. Haines' parish is Europe, from the tongue of the Bosporus to the coldest tip of Scandinavia.

One could be fooled by Wallace Haines. Is he an Englishman whose French is impeccable and devotion to the queen unquestionable?

No, he is an American transplant whose French is impeccable and whose love for things European is unquestionable, from Britain's royalty to the steelworker in Germany's industrial forests of stacks.

Some in Birmingham—Alabama, not England—remember decades ago when Wallace Haines

18

preached there. But for more than 20 years, he's been ministering in Europe as a catalyst who spurs contacts between other European Christian leaders.

Haines works through "the fellowship," that ubiquitous Washington-based group of believers whose assistance is given to everything from the Presidential Prayer Breakfast to Chuck Colson's prison ministry.

But Haines' years of residence in France and England, plus his constant movement over the whole of Europe, have given him the look, feel and appearance of a European.

Wallace Haines concentrates on helping Christians discover one another, forming themselves into fellowships, and involving nonbelievers with whom they ultimately share their witness. Eight members of the Parliament of a German-speaking country convene for prayer and fellowship regularly, with Wallace Haines' encouragement. In a nation on the edge of the Marxist East, a high government minister is inspired to form a group. In Islamic Turkey, an attorney who loves Christ and witnesses for him faithfully is strengthened as he imbibes the fellowship of one of the groups Haines has sparked. A small company of ambassadors are hosted by one of their number for dinner, in southern Europe. The focal point is Chuck Colson, there through the arrangements of Wallace Haines. But soon the concentration of the evening is Jesus Christ, not Colson.

* * *

The cold rain stabs like the emptying of a cloud of thumbtacks. A tiny nun sprints from the thousand-year-old convent near Bruges and waits for the Eklo bus. She is going home. If the bus is late, the train will leave without her.

We make light chatter, a salt and pepper blend of English and German, the best either of us can do. Wet droplets of rain give her habit the incongruous appearance of a sequined gown. She glances at her watch, a nervous rise on the edge of her laughter. The bus is late.

She steps from under the roadside shelter and peers far down the highway. A wake of water a mile away indicates the coming of something big. We squint, and see the fuzzy profile of a bus. She grabs her suitcase, and we exchange farewells. But the bus plummets by, dousing us in its wake. It wasn't the Eklo bus. Today the Eklo bus is late.

Now the 90-pound woman is worried. It is Saturday, and she may miss the last train. She won't sleep at her mother's home in France tonight if she misses the train. I'm getting a little concerned: if I miss the train to Brussels and the airport, I may not sleep in Alabama tonight. I'm going home too.

Suddenly the nun closes her habit around her face and hops to the curb. I can't believe it. She's got her thumb out, trying to hitchhike a ride to the train station. I am just as amazed that no one stops to pick up even a nun. The cars zip by her, the heads of their passengers glued on the street ahead, to avoid seeing the nun standing in the rain, as if leaving her there would be the depth of evil.

Finally she virtually steps into the path of a car. The befuddled driver squeals to a stop, she opens the door, tosses in her suitcase and I watch them fade down the highway toward Bruges.

Not long after, the Eklo bus lumbers up.

* * *

Of all the "faces of Europe"—resistance worker, businessman, politician, pastor, laborer—I recall the face of that tiny, rain-soaked nun most vividly.

There is something eerily symbolic about the nun and the cars passing her by. Is it the picture of Europe and the religious establishment of that part of the world? It would seem so. A close examination gives the impression that the church—like the nun—stands by the wayside, trying to get the attention of Europeans who seem not even to see her. If the nun is the symbol of the church in Europe, perhaps the picture of the average European is embodied in a Hannover laborer who has dropped out of the church so he won't have to pay the state-imposed church tax.

Europe stands at a crossroads of crisis. One direction leads back over what appears to be the narrow, rocky road to the culture which produced the Reformation and such spiritual giants as Luther, Zwingli, Calvin, Knox, the Wesleys, and Whitefield. The road ahead seems broad and inviting to Europe. It is curiously deceptive, its composition interwoven with Marxism, classical European socialism and a bit of capitalism, all laid out on the turf of humanist existentialism.

The problem of the church is a much more significant part of the crisis than the average European realizes. For the crisis of Europe now is a spiritual one. People like those described above know the direction to take. *But where will Europe go as it leaves the crossroads, and what will be the implications for Western civilization?*

CHAPTER TWO

Europe at the Crossroads

The old man, violin wedged between his chin and collarbone, raised his bow with the flare of a maestro readying to play at the Vienna Opera House. Actually, the dwarfish man's stage was a beer stand in the Zurich train station. His orchestra pit was a tall counter, where he had stationed a cassette tape player. A sign scribbled out the words, *"Kein Geld, bitte!"*—No money please.

As he prepared to strike the orchestra by pushing a button on the tape player, a drunk staggered toward the counter. Angrily, the violinist motioned him away; this was his moment on the stage, and no one else would share it.

The stage thus cleared, the violinist punched the button, and the tape machine began playing a merry German melody—the background for the old gentleman's violin solo. The fellow closed his creased eyelids, dusting the face of the violin with resin as the bow skimmed the strings. He was no longer in the Zurich train station. It was Europe of 50 years ago.

Lavishly festooned barons and baronnesses sat in a plush theater, listening to him play.

Other listeners had boarded his time machine, and were drifting back with him. Suddenly, a young man muttered, *"crazy!"* The time machine thudded to a hard crash with the solid earth of reality.

And the moment captured the dilemma of Europe.

The crossroads at which Europe stands is a critical intersection somewhere between the blissful hope of that old man and his music, and the hard, cynical reality of the young man whose song was a hard-spoken one-tone word: *Crazy.*

As she stands at the crossroads, Europe reminds one of a nervous grande dame, surrounded by the taunting hooligans of crisis, not the least of which is her defense itself. At no point since World War II has Europe been able to relax. Drive up to the small West German border town of Hof, and the towers and barbed wire which split the countryside speak too profoundly of that crisis. It is likewise signalled in a black Mercedes, racing down the autoban, bearing unusual yellow license plates. They represent one of the most ironic of Europe's situations. The passengers are Communist agents, spying on American troops, with their permission, just as Americans spy on Communist forces across the border, with permission of their enemies.

The disarray Europe feels is not helped by the fact that the Soviets have beefed up their ground troops in Eastern Europe by some 400,000 men in the last decade. They have similarly raised their tank strength; 20,000 of the monsters now snarl at the borders of

Western Europe. All the while, the North Atlantic Treaty Organization (NATO), charged with the defense of Western Europe, has suffered the loss of France, seen Italy cut its army by one-third, and watched Greece and Turkey—who once contributed 700,000 soldiers to NATO—go for each other's jugulars.

The more subtle, and hence more dangerous, crisis is political-philosophical-spiritual. All of these components combine to produce a rending tension which sends rifts and faults into every area of European life.

Communists, for example, are able to make gains as Europeans intensify their philosophical shift into humanism and their spiritual shift into materialism. By the mid-'70s, Italy's Communist Party had been able to win as much as 34 percent of the vote in national elections—only 9 percent short of the total which put Richard Nixon into the American presidency in 1968. The shocker is that many observers felt the strong influence of the Roman Catholic Church would hold back Marxist victories in Italy. But in a private conversation with a noted Englishman, Pope Paul estimated that one-third of the priests in Italy voted the Communist ticket in the national elections. A check with sources close to the Catholic Church in France and Spain confirmed that such a figure would likely be applied to those countries as well.

Some students of Europe insist there should be no great concern about the brand of Marxism evolving there, known as "Eurocommunism." It is, they say, simply an adaptation of the socialism most European nations have lived with for generations. Further, they suggest, the rise of Eurocommunists will add a touch of democracy and will not seriously affect cabinets in Western Europe.

Former Secretary of State Henry Kissinger disagrees. He does not believe the Communist parties of Western Europe are truly free from Moscow. Nor does he believe that they have strayed from the classical Marxist stance that the minority has the right to seize power and exercise control over the rest of the population. Thus he cannot accept the claims of Western European Communist leaders that they are interested in political pluralism.

Kissinger drew close to the heart of the problem when he said that "a relativist age debunks authority and puts nothing in its place as an organizing principle of society."[1] The crisis in authority is very much part of Europe's quandary as she stands at the crossroads. As she edges away from the deep religious convictions which held her fast for many generations, she searches for a new reality, sensing that soon she must make a commitment.

Perhaps it is her strong ties to the Christian faith in the past which makes her hard to reach now. Many Europeans, like many Americans, think they are "Christian" simply because they are European, baptized and a member of a state church. Evangelicals find that while 20,000 people per day are entering the church in Africa, the response rate in some parts of Europe is only one out of every 600 people. One evangelical leader described Europe as the world's most difficult mission field.

Statistics do little to help feel the pulse of the Christian efforts to win Europe. In Great Britain, there are massive monuments to Christian faith in the form of huge, ornate church buildings. But of the total population, only some 10 percent regularly attend church. Italy remains staunchly Roman Catholic— numerically anyway. But the authority of the church is in question for many, that erosion helped by the Communists and general anti-clericalism. There are some 100,000 Protestants. A fifth of the population of the Netherlands claims no church affiliation. Germany still has its strongholds of Christianity. In Nuremberg, on a Sunday morning, there are enough people walking to church, Bible in hand, to remind one of a town in the southern United States' Bible Belt. Belgium and Luxembourg are heavily Catholic—only 4 percent of their populations are Protestant. Among the French-speaking Walloons, there is a pronounced anti-clerical attitude. Some 99 percent of the population of France is baptized Roman Catholic, but there is a growing tide of feeling against the church, as France experiences a deepening of Marxism and humanism.

Part of the decline in religious interest may result from a slow return of economic concerns and problems. The boom of the postwar reconstruction period is leveling off. And another postwar boom is creating an employment problem. The "baby boom" which followed the war has thrust a wave of young adults on the beaches of the European job market, and the results are not good. Student riots in Italy in 1977 were sparked by the problem.

27

Thus, on every hand, it is clear Europe is on the road to change—whether it has selected a course for such change or not.

"This is a transition period like the Reformation, which fell between the medieval and the modern periods." The speaker was Dr. Penrose St. Amant, soon to retire as president of the Baptist seminary at Ruschlikon, a village not far from Zurich. "The Western world is going into a new epoch, described as post-modern. The modern era was characterized by the messianic dominance of science. Now there is much skepticism. People are worried about technology," said St. Amant.

As for Europe, "this is an old, but tired and sophisticated culture, half in hope, half in despair," said St. Amant. Immediately, the image of the old man and his violin and the young man and his cynicism, returns.

Werner Burklin is a realist with hope. As Youth for Christ's area director for Europe, Burklin knows the sadness and strength of Europe as a surgeon knows his patient. Burklin is a German. His assessment is based on a lifetime spent in Europe. "There is no doubt," he said, "that many people—especially young people—are moving away from postwar 'isms.' Many people have noted that materialism does not give them complete satisfaction; thus they are looking for spiritual values."

But that movement from secularism is hard for the average European, thinks Burklin. "It is quite difficult for them to make the jump from 'interest in the Gospel' and 'accepting the Gospel.' " Because of tradition, most Europeans regard themselves as Christians, so "it is difficult to make them aware of their need for a Savior," said Burklin.

Staffan Johansson feels that as Europe ponders the crossroads, there is a move away from materialism. Johansson sits at a writing table in his room at L'Abri, the assortment of chalets high in the Swiss Alps which comprise Francis Schaeffer's "shelter" for spiritual searchers. Johansson, a Swedish student, senses greater stress on quality of life rather than simply the acquisition of material strength which dominated European energies after World War II. But that quest for a better quality of life has only increased Europe's dilemma. "There is the realization that there must be something to base things on," says Johansson. The basic problem Europe must wrestle with is over what defines "quality."

Johansson is not optimistic that Europe will move in a truly constructive way. "There's not much readiness here to believe in anything. Americans will grab for anything as long as it works. But not the European. I don't see any motion in a good direction toward solid values," says the young Swede.

As Europe ponders the direction it will move from the crossroads, there are some stark shifts in its reference points—like the Catholic Church, as we've seen already. The situation of the church in Ireland is but one example.

"Ireland . . . is going through a powerful assessment of its national identity,"[2] said Bishop Cahal Daly of the Armagh Diocese. Part of the assessment

29

has to do with just how much impact the Catholic Church will continue to have on affairs and issues in Ireland. "The main harm," according to Posts and Telegraphs Minister Conor Cruise O'Brien, "is not that the church is tyrannical and overbearing, but that people tend to give lip service to things they don't believe in very much."[3]

Is this lack of belief characteristic of Europe as a whole? If it is, how could there be such a degeneration of faith in a land prayed and preached over by the Wesleys, Calvin, Luther, Zwingli and dozens of other "heroes of the faith"? How, indeed, did Europe arrive at this spiritual crossroads?

The ragged route to the crossroads begins in what seems another universe. All the alleyways and side streets which will become the route intersect at Augustine, the Bishop of Hyppo, in North Africa, who lived from 354 to 430. More specifically, they come together at the point of his great work, *The City of God,* written after the defeat of Rome in 410 A.D. Will Durant, in *The Story of Civilization: The Age of Faith,* says, "It was the first definitive formulation of the medieval mind."[4]

Augustine launched medieval thought at the bottoming out of the great tide of rationalism and reason which had swamped Rome in its classical period. Confidence in human reason had seemed ill-placed, humanity was looking for a new direction—just as Europe and the West searches now. As we shall see later, the despair of existentialism and nihilism growing out of World War II was over the massive betrayal of human reason which produced the death-technologies of war. So as Europe is now reacting against 20th-century rationalism and its associated barbarisms—like the slaughter of 12 million people in the War—might it not be possible Europe is sliding into a modern version of the medieval mind set? Should it not be the objective of the church in Europe to point the culture that way? The gross failure of the medieval era was in not striking balance between the qualitative role of faith and quantitative knowledge. Had this failure not occurred, it might be that by now, civilization would be enjoying technology under the Lordship of Christ—the only way an industrial state can survive without ultimately using its technology to commit suicide. But we're getting ahead of ourselves.

In *The City of God,* Augustine seemed, on occasion, to identify the church with the City of God. Later, the church would intensify this stress, and some of the results would be positive.

The medieval period—like America's Puritan age—has been much distorted in popular thinking. Obviously, life was not paradise, nor were values always on target, but there were some features needed desperately today. Lane Dennis, in *A Reason for Hope,* puts it this way:

> The distinctive social order of the High Middle Ages, which grew out of the Christian transformation of Western Europe, may be best described in terms of four preeminent features, namely: *community, significance, meaning,* and *wholeness.* These are important for our consideration, not only as a means to understand past

31

history, but more significantly, as a means for understanding the deficiencies of our own age, *for it is precisely these features which are so notably absent from our own culture, and so deeply longed for by modern man.* Moreover, the absence of these features in modern life affects not only personal, spiritual, and psychological well-being, but it is related to the greater crisis of our age, which includes potential ecological catastrophe and social collapse.[5]

When the United States Department of Housing and Urban Development began pushing the "New Town" concept, it was unwittingly urging a return to the medieval pattern. The so-called model communities, like Columbia, Maryland, and Reston, Virginia, were aimed at providing a community built around work opportunities close by, a wide economic variety and a sense of belonging. What they have lacked is the strong integrative point provided by the church in medieval society.

Will Durant writes about the medieval cathedral: "[It was] a home for their worship, a meeting place for their community, a school of letters for their children, a school of arts and crafts for their guilds, a Bible in stone whereby they might contemplate, in statue and pictures, the story of their faith. The house of the people was the house of God."[6] Thus the church and its attitudes and theology gave people in the Middle Ages sets of absolutes. Since the church was seen as the center of daily life, its authority extended into every area. As we noted earlier, many experts on Europe see the absence of a sense of absolutes as being at the heart of Europe's confusion of direction now.

If Augustine's thought would lead to a positive centrality of the church in the Middle Ages, there would also be some negative developments. For example, many Christians believe that the efforts to share Christ are hampered by the state church systems of some European nations. If one is baptized into the church in infancy because he is born a citizen of a certain country, it is hard later in life to actually lead him to a real relationship with Christ. Church taxes imposed by the state sometimes produce anti-clericalism, so that all presentations of the Gospel are automatically shut out. Again and again in conversations across Europe with evangelicals, the state church system was presented as a barrier to evangelism, not a help.

It is easy to see how what was a positive emphasis in Augustine became a negative. Wallace K. Ferguson and Geoffrey Brunn, in *A Survey of European Civilization,* describe the medieval priest like this: "He was a member of a great international institution, which was in itself a kind of state, superimposed on all secular states and having an administrative system, laws, property, and taxes of its own. The pope was the ruler of this state; the clergy were its officers; and the laymen in all Christian countries . . . were its subjects."[7] As the years passed, this great state which was the church would alter greatly. While the role of the church would diminish somewhat, the state church system would rise partly as an attempt to maintain the centrality of the church. Augustine's stress had led to a dominant role for the church in medieval society; it also provided a backdrop for the continuance of whatever dominance could be kept through state churches.

In the 13th century, the route to Europe's current crossroads began to curve at another milepost: the Renaissance. This milepost stands taller than others along the route to the crossroads, for it stands itself at an important intersection. As Europe hovered between the medieval period and the age of Renaissance, it contemplated a direction which would determine its stance in the present. For better or worse, the choice was made, and Europe took the first not-so-tentative steps down the road to her current crossroads.

The Renaissance began about the 13th century with a renewal of interest in the classics of Greece and Rome. A fresh discovery of Aristotle had been both a result and a cause of intensified interest. Said Will Durant:

> When a new race, after a millennium of barbaric darkness, found again the leisure and ability for speculation, it was Aristotle's "Organon" of logic . . . that would become the very mould of medieval thought, the strict mother of that scholastic philosophy which, though rendered sterile by encircling dogmas, nevertheless trained the intellect of adolescent Europe to reasoning and subtlety, constructed the terminology of modern science, and laid the bases of that same maturity of mind which was to outgrow and overthrow the very same system and methods which had given it birth and sustenance.[8]

It could be debated whether the way Aristotle's approach was later used really led to a "maturity of mind." In fact, there is ample evidence that a world enamored with Aristotle and his "concrete particulars" was the same one which exalted Mussolini for his punctual trains, made awards for technological achievement in the construction of better and bigger gas ovens, and led ultimately to the sterility of existentialism discussed more closely later on. "Aristotle preaches a return to things, to the 'unwithered face of nature' and reality; he had a lusty preference for the concrete particular, for the flesh and blood individual."[9]

The collision between Aristotle's method and the church, at first, was more like a meeting between two strangers who hoped to become friends. Roger Bacon, for example, is widely credited with being one of the moving scientific spirits as the Renaissance stirred to life. But Bacon was a Franciscan monk who wrote a work calling for a revolution in the sciences, at the request of Pope Clement IV. It is very true that the church made critical mistakes later on. The Franciscans condemned Bacon for his views, and the church slapped at Copernicus and Galileo for advancing the idea of a heliocentric solar system. But from the perspective of the 20th century and its life-and-death wrestling matches with pollution, nightmarish weapon systems, threats of biological research, one can only lament the rigid separation which developed between science/technology and theology/values!

As man's view of the church was changing during the Renaissance, so was his way of seeing himself.

Before, he had viewed himself against the backdrop of the church, with its powerful authoritative grasps on his life, defining, limiting, yet pressing him to reach for spiritual things. Now the new philosophy was urging him to lay hold on material things. Science would loose man from all the chains keeping him from soaring. Ultimately, Sir Francis Bacon would dream, in *The New Atlantis,* of a world in which science was in total control. "The End of Our Foundation is the Knowledge of Causes and secret motions of things; and the enlarging of the bounds of human empire, to the effecting of all things possible," wrote Bacon in *The New Atlantis.*

Man's new perspective on himself would later be called humanism. As a philosophy, it would wield great power over European minds, and would lie at the core of everything from Camus' *Plague* to Nietzsche's Superman.

The implications for the European church were staggering. Thomas Aquinas and the Schoolmen sought to weld a sturdy seam between Aristotle's natural science and theology. The result was "natural theology," a seam which strengthened the philosophy of nature, but one which could not, under the greatest of stress, hold together the budding materialism of the Renaissance and the sterile theology of the Age of Faith. "As philosophy and theology moved continually beyond Aquinas, no more would the mystery of the universe be approached solely by means of Revelation, theology, Scripture, the Church," says Lane Dennis.[10]

The church's response sometimes led to an increasing secularization of itself. At least in style of government and its own accumulation of material wealth, it was coming more to resemble culture. But at the same time, it was withdrawing deeper into itself, isolating morality and values from daily life. The result of all this was a loss of respect for the church. Certainly it was no longer feared. But the crisis was deeper: Neither was it revered.

The slide was checked—but not stopped—by the Reformation. While important reforms resulted from that movement, there were some ways in which the Reformation actually contributed to the condition in which the European church found itself in the 20th century. The Lutheran and Reformed Churches which grew out of the Reformation became state churches. Further, "The Reformation emphasis upon the importance of individual faith devalued the importance of the Church as the body of Christ, and fragmented the unity of the Church into a host of warring sects."[11]

The route out of the Reformation period led squarely to the roosts of the French revolutionists—Voltaire, Rousseau. Voltaire—whom Victor Hugo likened as the embodiment of the 18th century—was by no means an atheist. But his faith, such as it was, perceived God in broad, impersonal categories. He considered himself a theist, yet the church had no place in Voltaire's scheme of things.

During the Revolution, Rousseau at one time toyed with the idea of creating a new religion. Like Voltaire, he saw some of the value of constraints the church could offer society. But for Rousseau—and this would echo later in Hitler—the Christian religion was too "weak." The French Revolution, after all, rested on the bedrock of human reason, and Rousseau could not then see the flaws and faults cutting through that bedrock. The last thing he wanted was a religious system that would suggest that man could not function without recognizing his limitations.

Is this the stirring of the utilitarianism which would someday be the philosophy of so much of Europe toward the church? For Rousseau, the church *might* be a handy revolutionary tool. For many Europeans, it is now a nifty social tool—for weddings, funerals, confirmations.

In the 19th century, all the cancerous attitudes toward the church which had been building in Europe for 600 years produced an outbreak of tumors. The 19th century saw the rise of Wagner, who believed the German people to be the redeemers of the world and his art the tools of salvation. There was Nietzsche, seeking to write God's obituary. Darwin and the theory of evolution would contribute to the sickness of attitude about the church. And of course Marx emerged, teaching that the church was the lackey of the ruling classes, and predicting its demise in the revolutions to come.

It is little wonder that in the 20th century the church in Europe stands at a crossroads! It has been moving this way for 700 years.

There is an immense irony here, one the United States must not ignore. It was Europe which became the depository of the Gospel. Without the strong faith which characterized her early history, Europe would have had nothing to pass on to the New World. There would have been no Pilgrims, no Puritans, no powerful preaching traditions. The great Christian denominations which enrich American life would not exist—there would have been no Wesleys to lay the foundations of Methodism, no John Knox or John Calvin to spur the Presbyterians, no Anabaptist tradition to help form the more than 25 Baptist groups. The educational institutions in America, which have grown to be among the most important in the world, would not have existed—they were the children of the denominations. Indeed, one wonders what America would have been without Europe's strong Christian tradition. And the irony is that now Europe is one of the world's most needful mission fields.

CHAPTER THREE

Europe's Spiritual Pulsebeat:
The West

Recent headlines about youth in Italy, Germany and England are worrisome.

For Italian radical youth, even the Communists are too tame. Boiling in towering thunderheads of unemployment, their solution is a non-solution. Destroy what is. That is the plan, in toto.

They are joined spiritually by the terrorist gangs of West Germany. An industrialist is kidnapped. The aim of the perpetrators is to throw society into chaos. Anarchy is the objective. The forms must be brought down, they say.

In England, mother-country of 1970s rock music, a new form has emerged: Punk rock. The form's "artisans" make obscene noises and sing offensive lyrics. It is no longer the music of rage, protest and revolution. It is the music of disgust.

And at London's Notting Hill, 233 people are injured when young black people from the Caribbean and the police battle it out.

In Northern Ireland, a young man deftly pulls together the wires of a bomb . . .

The International Herald-Tribune announces that French business leaders are meeting with Marxist chiefs. The announcement reeks of fatalism. The Communists have made such gains in French municipal elections that it has become clear to the business people that they must get to know the Marxists a bit better.

Yet . . . Paris bubbles with chatter about the "New Philosophers," a group of young leftists who are attacking Marxism. Andre Gluckmann, a leader of the new movement describes it as "refusal to be swept along the rails of a system that was issued 150 years ago by an illustrious longbeard."[1] Henri Levy is the pessimist. "We are realizing that the twentieth century's great invention may prove to be the concentration camp," he says. "The only successful revolution of this century is totalitarianism. The Soviet prison camp is Marxist, as Marxist as Auschwitz was Nazi," he says.[2]

Yet the New Philosophers are not Christian. With France, they stand at the crossroads.

Statistically, France seems quite "religious." Eighty-five percent of her people claim they are Roman Catholic. Eleven cardinals, 117 bishops and more than 47,000 priests make up the hierarchy of the Roman Catholic Church in France.

But the truth is that only 21 percent practice their faith on a regular basis. Sociologist Pierre Vilain breaks it out like this:

- 33 percent of the French people are non-practicing Catholics;
- 28 percent of the people are Catholics, again non-practicing, who do not accept the deity and role of Christ;
- 21 percent are practicing believers;
- 12 percent have no religion;
- 6 percent belong to other religions.

A report prepared by World Vision for the International Congress on World Evangelism, describes the "de-christianization" of France:

> Fully ten million French "believers" over 20 years of age have rejected the Church except for life's "sacramental" experiences (marriage, baptism, death). These ten million have tailored for themselves a "personalized" religion. Twenty-five percent of these ten million quit the Church before 16 years of age, from 16 to 30 another 36 percent drop out. For fully two-thirds of these, the drop-out was because professional life and family life absorbed everything. Church just faded away, it was no longer important. Only one in five dropped the Church because of conscious objections.

There are maybe 800,000 Protestants in France. The World Vision report thinks about 180,000 of them may be churchgoers. "Today virtually no significant aspect of French life lacks a 'Protestant presence' in its roster of important people. Unfortunately this has tended to cut off the Protestant church from the masses," says the report.

Juan and Maria Cortez exist in Roman Catholic Spain like microbes on the back of an elephant. In 1974, their country had a population of 34,551,345. *The Catholic Almanac* that year said that 34,162,178 of the Spaniards were Catholic. Juan and Maria were not among them.

Maria, though a Spaniard, was educated at a home operated by Baptists in Rome. Her husband studied at the Baptist seminary at Ruschlikon, Switzerland. Natives of Valencia, they wound up in Nuremberg, Germany, as "guestworkers." They paid no rent for their fifth-floor apartment. Maria earned it by waxing the stairwell.

On Sunday afternoons, she and Juan convened more Spanish "guestworkers" in Germany at a gargantuan church where Luther's ally Melanchthon worshipped hundreds of years ago. The building swallowed up the tiny group of people.

Later, Juan and Maria and many of their friends became part of an English-speaking Baptist congregation meeting in a furniture warehouse in the Nuremberg suburb of Furth. Juan taught a Sunday School class in Spanish, using literature from the Southern Baptist Spanish publishing house in El Paso, Texas. Maria, who speaks eight languages, translated the pastor's sermons for the Spaniards in the church.

Thirteen of their countrymen received Christ through that ministry.

The Protestant church in Spain was burned in the firestorms of the Inquisition in the 16th century. For 300 years, Protestants lived in perpetual danger.

There was a brief revival of Protestantism in 1868, but folllowing the Civil War, in 1939, Protestant churches were closed. Then, in 1968, the Law of Religious Liberty granted legal recognition to Protestants.

The Plymouth Brethren, with 5,000 members, is the largest evangelical group in Spain. It is followed by the Spanish Evangelical Baptist Union, also with a membership of about 5,000. Third is the Federation of Independent Evangelical Churches, with about 3,000 members. Two-thirds of Spain's Protestants belong to those three bodies.

John Haggai is an American evangelist who walks the world as if he were born everywhere. Of Syrian descent, Haggai has a unique way of bridging east and west as effectively as the spans across the Bosporus.

Still, there was wariness on the part of some when it was announced that Haggai would conduct mass evangelism crusades in Portugal in 1972. Like neighboring Spain, the Roman Catholic Church lays claim to some 90 percent of the population—though only about half of the people are seriously involved in the church.

Up to 1967, there had been severe restrictions on the use of public buildings in Portugal for evangelism efforts. Haggai's was the first massive test of a relaxation of restrictions. The results were impressive. Night after night, the halls in Lisbon and Oporto where Haggai preached were jammed. Thousands of decisions were made for Christ. Haggai established rapport with some segments of Portuguese official-dom.

Evangelical work in Portugal had been seeded in the 19th century by members of the diplomatic corps from Germany and England. In 1839, a Spaniard, Dr. Vicente Gomes y Togar, established the first evangel-ical preaching mission. In the 1870s, British Breth-ren, Anglicans, Methodists and Baptists all estab-lished work.

Since 1933, there has been an increase of Bible conferences throughout Portugal. Some 2,000 people attend the conferences every year.

The Assemblies of God comprise the largest evan-gelical group in Portugal, with 7,500 members, fol-lowed by Seventh-day Adventists and the Baptists.

I was on a collision course with the biggest Russian I'd ever seen. A friend and I had been dodging through the crowds at an Italian department store. I had recently arrived in Europe as pastor of an English-speaking congregation. I wanted to miss nothing and twisted my head in every direction. I didn't see the mountainous man until we had almost bumped.

There could be no question but that he was a Rus-sian. His Slavic head was sandwiched between a Solzhenitsyn-beard, sans mustache, and a black fur cap. No way he could be anything but a Russian.

Then my friend called out, "Glenn, it's good to see you." The next thing I knew I was meeting my first Russian who was no Russian at all. A voice came out of that finely contoured European face, with the accents of Alabama! The man was Glenn Vernon, youth director for the European Baptist Convention—the body I would serve through. Glenn was in Italy for the same meeting my friend and I had come to attend.

The European Baptist Convention is one of several bodies and individual churches in Europe to minister to Americans overseas. Some 40 churches are aligned with the European Baptist Convention—which is a "fraternal" body of the Southern Baptist Convention in the United States.

The churches aiming their ministries at Americans in European cities sometimes focus on as many people as a church in an American community. In Nuremberg, for example, during the period I served there in the mid-1960s, there were some 40,000 Americans, mostly servicemen and their families.

The EBC conducts a bustling life of its own. It bears down heavily on mission support. In the summer, there is a Europe-wide retreat at Interlaken, Switzerland. Youth retreats for American dependents are conducted regularly. The churches undertake visitation programs typical of Baptists, though they often find it difficult to penetrate military housing areas, which prohibit solicitation of any kind.

Frequently, the EBC churches touch Europeans, as well as Americans. There were, for example, two sisters who attended our church in Nuremberg every Sunday. They spoke no English, and could not even give a greeting to their fellow parishioners.

Soon, I had established a pattern of visiting the sisters—both elderly—on Tuesdays. I would carry a church bulletin with me, and explain what had happened on the previous Sunday. Their apartment was a depressing two rooms on the back of an ancient structure. A thick wall blocked out any sunshine which might have otherwise slipped into their sitting room-kitchen.

I often wondered what the women had experienced, as I sat in their apartment. Nuremberg had been bombed heavily during the war. I thought of them crouching in this same flat as the bombers thundered overhead. And they had a brother who now lived in South America. I could only muse over why he had left Germany for a place so far away. But their best memories were recent ones. Every Tuesday they told again how they had gone to hear Billy Graham preach at Nuremberg's Soldiers Field—the same place where Hitler had reviewed his troops.

One Sunday, the sisters left the church in a great stew. Something had gone wrong, and they both were disturbed. The next week I found out why. The pianist, that Sunday morning, had unwittingly chosen for her postlude a hymn set to the same tune as *Deutschland Uber Alles*—the anthem loved by Hitler . . .

Many observers feel the Roman Catholic Church has been thoroughly liberalized by Vatican II and the events following it. This liberalizing trend has dug deeply into the Catholic Church in the Netherlands. In fact, liberal priests and bishops in the late 1960s and early 1970s were in as seething a stew as Archbishop Lefebvre, the extremely conservative French Catholic.

48

Nearly 40 percent of the Dutch population is Roman Catholic. Protestants make up about 30 percent of the population. Twenty-two percent of the Dutch people have no church connections. Forty-three percent do not own a Bible or even possess a portion of the Scripture.

That despite government encouragement of religion. There is official support for three school systems—one for Catholics, one for Protestants, one for people who prefer no religious instruction. The government provides television time for religious groups.

The war years were heroic for the Dutch Reformed Church. Christian leaders were speaking out boldly against Nazi injustices. But after the war, the surge of revival faded as the Dutch joined the rest of Europe in a pursuit of secularity.

Now the ordered gentleness of Dutch life has been shattered. Terrorism has collided with tranquility.

Protestants in Belgium have been working at getting together. The union of three churches was to be completed by 1978. The denominations were the Protestant Church of Belgium, the Reformed Church of Belgium and the *Gereformeerde Kerken in Belgie*.

The new church was expected to have 35,000 members—40 percent of all Belgian Protestants. There would be 113 parishes.

The Protestant Church of Belgium dates from the Reformation. When the Spaniards conquered Belgium in 1604, Protestants were forced underground, and the church ceased to influence the nation measurably. Then, in 1839, 16 Protestant church groups combined into a "Union of Churches." In 1957, this group became the Evangelical Protestant Church of Belgium. In 1969, there was another merger, this time between the Methodists and the Evangelical Church, and the Protestant Church of Belgium was born.

In 1837, the Belgian Evangelical Society was born. The church which grew out of that in 1849 was called the Belgian Christian Missionary Church. In 1969, it became the fiercely independent Reformed Church. That hunger for independence has not halted it from pursuing merger with the other churches.

"The smallest and newest of the churches," explains *Carillon*—the news bulletin of the Protestant Church of Belgium—"is the *Gereformeerde Kerken,* which arose from evangelical work of the *Gereformeerde Kerken* in Holland at the end of the nineteenth century. . . It has about 2,000 members; due to its traditional emphasis on evangelism, over half of these members are now Belgian."

The Rev. Bruce E. Shields, of the Institute for the Study of Christian Origins, Tübingen, Germany, tells the story of Frau "Schmidt":

"Frau Schmidt is Dina Luik's Avon lady. In 1973, Scott Bartchy (also of the Institute staff) was asked to counsel with her teenage son in prison. . . Then we lost contact with him, only to hear later that he had been found dead of a lethal mixture of drugs and alcohol. . . Fred Norris and I attended the funeral in May. The Lutheran pastor knew he was not really wanted there, since the mother had lost her faith in God because of the tragedy; but he not only went through the motions of the burial service, but also preached a sermon telling us we had no right to question the ways of God. The sermon was brought to an abrupt (but somehow appropriate) end, when the mother raised her fist and shouted, 'There is no righteous God!'

"Since then Dina has maintained her contact with Frau Schmidt, seeing her through a nervous breakdown and bouts with alcoholism, tolerating her inconsistent denials of God, and loving her back to real life. . .

"Early in November, Dina had a strange conversation with Frau Schmidt which surprised even her. Over the months Frau Schmidt had learned some things about our congregation: that our members are all believers, that they were baptized as believers, and that they had left the state church. It soon became apparent, however, that she thought that before she could even visit for a service she must decide to be baptized and withdraw her membership in the state church. This sort of misunderstanding is not unusual, since we are known as a group who really believes in something. However, Dina made it clear to her that anybody is welcome to attend our services, and she added her testimony that her family had attended for a long time before coming to a decision.

"So last night she came with Dina to the Bible study in our apartment. . . I was just interrupted by a telephone call from Dina, in which she described

Frau Schmidt's positive reaction to the Bible study. . . She wants to schedule a future session in her apartment, if we'll come.''

"What we are witnessing here in Gothenburg is the nearest thing to a genuine revival of religion that I have seen in a long time." The speaker was Billy Graham. The city was in Sweden.

The critics had said it would never happen—not in gloomy Sweden, the country with the highest suicide rate in the Western world. Church attendance has plummeted into a deep valley of apathy. Sweden's reputation for sexual permissiveness is known throughout the world. There have been strong tides of anti-Americanism.

But the 14,000-seat arena is filled every night. Hundreds wait outside in the snowy evening. At the invitation by the evangelist to make a decision for Christ, hundreds move forward.

Says the Lutheran Bishop of Gothenburg: "Billy Graham has taught us a lesson in evangelism. If he ever returns, he will have much greater church support."

The Vikings infested the world like a deadly, fast-spreading disease. Hardly any warning was more fearful to coastal villages of the early Middle Ages than the shout that the Vikings were coming. But the Vikings were unwittingly transporting back to their lands a powerful antidote to their savagery—the Christian faith.

As the raiders brought back slaves to Norway,

there were often a few Christians among the human baggage. Even bishops and priests were captured and brought to Norway. Slowly, they began to win their captors to the Christian faith.

As Norway's political life developed, the king emerged as supreme in all things, both temporal and spiritual. Thus it was by royal decree that the Reformation came to Norway, and Roman Catholic bishops were replaced—by order of the king—by "evangelical superintendents."

In 1814, the Constitution stipulated that the Evangelical Lutheran Church would be the official state religion. Parliament was the legislative body of the church, and the king appointed clergy. In 1845, a law permitted Norwegians to join other church groups if they wished. But the state church was retained.

Some 95 percent of the population are members of the state church. Children are automatically given training in Christianity in the elementary schools, unless parents object. Pastors have further opportunity to reach youngsters through classes preparing them for Confirmation.

There are free church movements within Norway. About 36,000 people belong to churches not affiliated with the state church. Pentecostals are strong, having sent out about 200 missionaries.

Ninety-nine percent of the people of Finland claim to be Christian. As in other Nordic countries, Lutheran Orthodoxy is the state religion. The state church is governed by a Synod of 108 members. Two-thirds of them are laypeople.

There is a church tax, collected by the state, a service paid for by the church. The church keeps the records on its members. The state permits religious instruction of elementary school pupils, in line with the denomination with which the majority is affiliated. There are chaplains in the military and in prisons.

A zesty, crusade-minded Christianity swept Finland in 1050. In 1527, a clamp was placed on the political power of the bishops. The Reformation proceeded smoothly, and by 1593, the Lutheran faith became official doctrine.

Finland has been a land of many revival movements, including one that began about 1960. Stress in all these movements has been toward personal pietism, resulting in home worship and small group fellowships. In urban areas, church attendance is between 10 percent and 15 percent. In rural sections, it may be as high as 30 percent.

Two thousand years after the Apostle Paul preached on Athens' Mars Hill, 8.5 million of Greece's 9 million people are claimed by the Greek Orthodox Church. Even in a pluralistic country like the United States, the Greek Orthodox Church maintains a powerful ethnic orientation in Greek communities. Tragically, there is evidence that many Greeks do not understand the basic truths of Christianity, and are affiliated with the Church for ethnic or traditional reasons.

Greece was the first country in Europe where the Gospel took root. But many non-Orthodox would today find a strong variance between that early Christianity and the present religion.

The World Vision profile of Greece put it this way:

> The influence of the ancient hellenistic religions. . .cannot be ignored. When Constantine declared Christianity to be the official religion of the Roman Empire (including Greece) in the early 4th century, there was still a widespread and deep belief in a complex system of pagan deities, folk religion and superstition. An already polytheistic people had little difficulty accepting the new names of Christianity and adapting them to their existing beliefs. For example, many scholars and theologians hold that the pagan virgin goddess Athena was simply replaced by a Christian virgin "goddess," Mary. Other remnants of pre-Christian tradition are still evident in the worship forms of many of the people. Nearly every village has its own local witch, and many ancient superstitious rituals are still performed.

There is powerful opposition to non-Orthodox bodies in Greece. Understandably, then, the evangelical community is small—only about 15,000 people. The Greek Evangelical Church, with about 5,000 members, is the largest of these groups. There are also about 5,000 members of the Fellowship of Free Evangelical Churches. Four Pentecostal groups number some 2,000.

Malcolm Muggeridge, called by some pundits "St. Mugg," in view of his turn to Christianity, has hope. Muggeridge recently said:

There will be a breakdown. Out of that breakdown will be a form of authoritarianism that is anti-Christian. These will be great testing times. But I don't feel at all hopeless. Where is the Church strongest? In Poland, which is a Communist country. And out of Russia, where religion is viciously persecuted, has come Solzhenitsyn, a man who speaks the language of Western civilization. So the faith will survive. The times will be hard, but God is on the side of those who worship Him, and His people will prevail. . . . No, I don't feel at all hopeless."[3]

CHAPTER FOUR

Europe's Spiritual Pulsebeat: The East

There are twice as many Baptists in the Communist countries of Europe than in Western Europe, reports the Baptist World Alliance (BWA).

In 1977, the BWA found that there were 28,395 more Baptists in Europe than in 1976. Slightly more than 64 percent of these—or 753,623—were in the eight countries where Communists are in power. There are 418,441 Baptists in Western Europe. Carl W. Tiller, BWA associate secretary says it's been that way for some time.

The Soviet Union has more Baptists than any other nation in Europe, with 545,000. Romania is third, with 164,000. That nation has been increasing in its Baptist population by about 20,000 a year every year since 1972.

Baptist work in East Germany surprises many who have concluded that there is no possibility of witness in that walled society.

"The work in East Berlin is allowed for all

groups—the children, young people, and adults as well," says Luther Morphis, a veteran missionary to West Berlin. "They carry on the work very much as they desire within the church building,"[1] he continues.

There are limitations on the kind of work they can do on the outside. But those restrictions do not prevent the operation of a Baptist Book Store in East Berlin—the only one in the Communist bloc. The store sells Christian books published in East Germany, printed under government authorization, as are all books there. The books include the Bible.

"They are able to ship books into other Eastern countries, where it is not possible to get books from the West. The involvement of the book store is quite extensive, and it is a very real opportunity of getting the Word of God, as well as religious books, into the hands of people in different countries,"[2] Morphis says.

There are some 300 book tables scattered in Baptist churches in East Germany. The book store sends publications directly to the churches for display.

Dr. Denton Lotz believes Western Christians have much to learn from their brothers and sisters in Eastern Europe. Lotz is a professor at the Baptist seminary at Ruschlikon, Switzerland. His heartbeat is East Europe, where he visits frequently.

"The first thing we can learn from our brethren in Eastern Europe," says Lotz, "is the centrality of Scripture. Have we in the West not lost a certain sense of discipline in responding to the authority of

Scripture?" he wonders. "I remember when studying in Gottingen, Germany, that Professor J. Jeremias always used to say, 'Have no fear of those who you think would destroy the Bible. The power is there and you can't get away from it.' In a very clear way this has been shown to me in country after country, whether at a pastor's conference in Warsaw, Poland, or a Bible study in Bucharest, Romania, or a worship service in Prague, Czechoslovakia. It is almost as though the Church has sprung up 'out of nothing' until one realizes they had the Bible," says Lotz.

The stress on prayer as a daily encounter with God is a second factor Lotz thinks Christians in the West can learn from those in the East. He says: "I have stood for two hours or more at prayer meetings where 50 or more people have prayed. I am amazed to meet peasants who are illiterate, but then when they prayed I was aware of a very sensitive and deep soul. If prayer for many of us has only been a 'crisis' experience, our brethren teach us that the continual life of a Christian is crisis and, thus, prayerful."

"Finally," Lotz continues, "we could learn that commitment to Christ takes priority over everything else." In Eastern Europe, "commitment to Christ might mean that following him is more important than my job. It might mean giving up social advancement, or acceptance by the crowd. To be a committed Christian means to give to the utmost in spite of the personal costs. I have known men and women who worked all day, and then from 5 in the afternoon until 10 at night work on building a church for two years straight," says Lotz.

Lotz believes that the job of evangelism in Communist Europe will be done best by Christians who live there. He acknowledges the difficulty and restrictions, and believes Western Christians can contribute the most by doing what helps Christians in the Marxist nations. "You can buy a Bible in Warsaw, Poland, and East Berlin, or in Prague, Budapest and elsewhere," he says. "The two places that need Bibles the most (Russia and Romania) have greater restrictions. But we prefer to work openly and officially through diplomatic channels with the United Bible Society to get permission to import the Bibles. The Romanian government has allowed 10,000 Bibles to be brought into the country. This is just a beginning. I understand the Russian Baptists are getting permission to print some New Testaments," Lotz observes.

But the way is not easy. Peter Deyneka Jr., General Director of the Slavic Gospel Association, tells the story of Misha, a seven-year-old Russian boy:

"At school he was under intense pressure for months to join the Octobrists, a Communist club for children seven to nine years old, devoted particularly to Lenin. In the face of this pressure, he courageously refused to join. But his teachers determined to make him conform.

"One day Misha's oldest sister, Tanya, came running home from school. She cried out to her parents, 'They're going to make Misha join the Octobrists and put on the Lenin pin!'

"Misha's father rushed back to the school. But he

couldn't find his little boy anywhere. Then he saw a group of children marching into the club room. He looked inside. He saw children marching up to have the Lenin emblem pinned on their shirts. This ceremony meant they were becoming Octobrists.

"Then the father saw some older students pushing a little boy onto the stage. It was Misha—frightened, looking around for help, finding none. The father could only pray with a hurting heart and watch, with tears in his eyes. He knew he couldn't stop the ceremony, for he might be arrested for disrupting a public meeting.

"The father watched as Misha jerked away from an older student who was about to pin the Lenin emblem on the little boy's shirt. Another student tried to pin on the emblem. Misha turned and fled from the stage. Roars of derisive laughter from students and teachers followed the little boy every step of the way. It was a moment of terrible humiliation for Misha—but also a moment of great courage.

"Still, Misha's father could not go to the little boy and hug him tightly to himself. To avoid further trouble, he knew he must wait until he and Misha were at home alone.

"Misha's father told me, 'As we send our children off to school, we know they're stepping out into a hostile world. We know they are often pressured and ridiculed. We know they're being questioned repeatedly by authorities. And we know what they say to those who question them could even cause our children to be taken away from us.' "

Rochunga Pudaite has a vision: To put Bibles in the hands of the world's masses. That includes the millions who live in the Soviet Union.

Through a friendship pact existing between India and Russia, Pudaite and his organization, Bibles for the World, are sending 10,000 Bibles per month to the Soviet Union.

Under the pact, Bibles can be mailed legally as "cultural" books. The agreement to ship the Bibles was made in 1971; for a 10-year period. But, says Pudaite, "we must print all we can while this door is open." Entertainer Pat Boone has spearheaded a drive in the United States to raise funds for the project.

According to a Soviet dissident, there's a surge of interest in religion on the part of Russian youth. M. Meerson-Aksenov, writing in *Diakonia,* a publication of Forham University's Center for Eastern Christian Studies, says the revival of religious interest stems back to the early 1960s. He is an Orthodox Christian, and the renewed interest he writes about centers largely on that tradition.

But, he says, the revival spreads to all religious groups, including Jews. Within Christianity, the youth have combined a number of forms from several different Christian bodies, producing a "confessional syncretism."

"A poll taken by a priest among the oppositionist intelligentsia in the capital (Moscow) showed that of 100 persons only three called themselves atheists, the rest in one degree or another declared themselves believers,"[3, 4] writes Meerson-Aksenov.

Like other dissident forms within the Soviet Union, there is the production of religious *samizdat,* or self-published material.

The anonymous writer may have been prophetic without knowing it.

His article appeared in the January, 1977, issue of *World Vision.* He was describing the status of Christianity in Hungary. "In Hungary a key person in church/state relationships is the Government-appointed President of the Free Churches, Sandor Palotai," he wrote. Then the writer reported about allegations of "bribery and corruption" brought against Palotai by some of his fellow churchmen. The leader of the protests against Palotai, the Rev. Tibor Ivanyi, a Methodist, was dismissed.

Observed the *World Vision* writer: "The affair underlined the way in which the West can, often unwittingly, be taken in by claims of religious freedom in such countries as Hungary. Undoubtedly, official church visitors to East European countries are severely restricted in their ability to make objective assessments, because visits are carefully orchestrated."

Thus the question: Was Billy Graham's appearance in Hungary in the fall of 1977 part of this effort at "careful orchestration?" Palotai had sat on the platform of a Billy Graham crusade in the United States. That prompted the *World Vision* writer, in January of 1977, to quote a Budapest pastor: "If Billy Graham has welcomed Palotai to the United States, perhaps

Palotai will feel under obligation to invite Dr. Graham to Hungary!''

There was also the political factor. Hungarian government boss Janos Kadar was known to be interested in winning for his country a "most favored nation" trade standing with the United States. There had been disquiet in the United States as well as Hungary over Kadar's repression of the church—it was in Hungary, after all, that Cardinal Mindszenty had had to seek asylum in the United States legation for 15 years. Nevertheless, following Graham to Hungary in 1977 were three high ranking American Catholic bishops.

Whatever the case, the Gospel was preached in Hungary. On the first day of his preaching in the country, Graham faced a crowd of 10,000, gathering outdoors near the Danube. There had been no massive secular publicity, but the throng assembled anyway. When the invitation was given, thousands raised their hands indicating they wanted to rededicate themselves to Christ.

Graham's official host was indeed Palotai's Council of Free Churches.

That group numbers about 50,000 Protestants, and is a definite minority in the country. Both the Reformed and Lutheran bodies are larger. When the Communists came to power after World War II, Hungary was two-thirds Roman Catholic. Even now, 65 percent of the Hungarians claim membership in the Roman Catholic Church. Twenty percent fall into categories classified as Protestant. The rest are Eastern Orthodox and Jewish.

"Rarely does one get a chance to help make history—as well as celebrate it—in one event."

So World Vision President Stanley Mooneyham described his feelings as he participated in the opening, on October 31, 1976, of the first Protestant Faculty of Theology in the Balkans named after Croatian reformer Matija Vlacic Illirik, a contemporary of Martin Luther. "Flacius [the Latinized version of his name] is to the Slavs what Luther is to the Germans," says Mooneyham.

It is difficult to really understand just how significant the establishment of the Faculty is, says Mooneyham, without knowing some of the religious background of Yugoslavia, where the school is located, in the city of Zagreb.

Protestant evangelicals are the tiniest of minorities in the country. Of a population of 21 million, there are perhaps 125,000 of them. The Roman Catholics number six million, the Moslems a half million. There are 110,000 people in the Lutheran and Reformed churches. That leaves 15,000, divided among Baptists, Methodists, Pentecostals and Brethren, Mooneyham notes.

Though there were Protestant Bible schools, there was no graduate theological faculty for evangelicals. Consequently, they studied at Roman Catholic or Orthodox institutions.

"The need for a theological training center can hardly be overstated," Mooneyham says.

Dr. Josip Horak, president of the Baptist Union, and Senior Wladimir Deutsch, a Lutheran pastor in Zagreb, were the movers behind the graduate theological faculty. "Their dream for a theological center with evangelical warmth and academic excellence was given stimulus at the Lausanne Congress in 1974," Mooneyham was told by Dr. Hrak.

It seemed clear God's hand was on the effort from the beginning. Leaders from other churches joined the project. Facilities were provided by the Lutheran Church of Croatia, and the government gave approval to the institution as a five-year theological institution on the university level.

Writing to Mooneyham, World Vision European director Ralph Hamburger stated: "Many problems will have to be overcome, but that is nothing new to them. They are reconstructed men. They have an adequate building. They have a beginning teaching staff. They have an eager number of students. They have the first evidences of financial partnership. They are going to run with that, warm in spirit, expecting God to lead."

In summary, it is interesting and ironic to note that Christian advance in Western Europe, with its opportunity and relative freedom, lags behind that of Eastern Europe, with its monumental obstacles. It is a repeat of the most ancient Christian history. When the price of following Christ is heaviest to bear, when popular acceptance of the faith is at its lowest, there seems to be the brightest glowing of the fires of the church. That is an encouraging word for believers throughout the world who may face increasing persecution in years to come.

CHAPTER FIVE

Reflections on Europe

The lanky Finnish schoolboy hardly had time to concentrate on things religious. He was a church member who even attended. But his aim was to work out a non-combative, "peaceful co-existence" kind of relationship with God. Other things occupied center stage. Like athletics—his father was a gold medalist at the 1932 Olympics and brought back to Finland a silver medal in 1936. And the young man loved the tangles of student government. There was always his social life to gobble up spare time.

Hardly a beginning for a man who would become director of one of the largest evangelical movements to aim at winning Europe to Christ. But that described the early years of Kalevi Lehtinen, the man who leads a staff of 300 people as European director of Campus Crusade for Christ.

It was through his involvement with student government affairs that Lehtinen committed his life to Christ. While helping organize a Christian conference at his school, he was stricken with the different lifestyle of the believers. Through their influence, he received Christ, and, at age 17 decided to pursue a Christian vocation.

In 1964, after graduating from the University of Helsinki, Lehtinen was ordained a Lutheran minister. In 1966, he heard Campus Crusade President Bill Bright speak at the World Congress on Evangelism in Berlin. Bright's spirit attracted him, and he was open when a Campus Crusade representative contacted him in a short time. He moved quickly through a variety of jobs—director of the ministry in Finland, special representative in Europe, European coordinator for training, regional director for Germany, the Netherlands, Switzerland and Belgium. In 1977, he was named Campus Crusade's director of affairs for Europe.

Campus Crusade's work in Europe was only one year old when, in 1967, Lehtinen and his wife, Eine, joined the staff. "Only Iceland and Belgium and Malta are notable countries without staff at present," Lehtinen says. By the summer of 1977, the staff throughout Europe had grown to 350, with 80 percent of them European nationals.

The budget for Campus Crusade's ministry in Europe is about one million dollars. "Over 75 percent of this money will be raised in Europe, and the rest will come from our central source in the United States," says Lehtinen. Like all aspects of Campus Crusade, persons working in the European ministry must raise their own support. However, staff members in the United States raise an extra 17 percent which goes into a central fund at Campus Crusade's California headquarters.

From that central source, money is available for administrative expenses and the foreign ministries of Campus Crusade. "The money raised in Europe will come almost exclusively through the national ministries, and will be raised as small contributions within the countries. Our European staff raise their salaries basically within Europe. In the beginning, we give a new staff member a subsidy from our central funds. But after a period of two to three years, and in some countries longer, every staff member is responsible for his own support," says Lehtinen.

When it comes to winning Europeans to Christ, Lehtinen sees wide variation between countries in the response rate. "Countries with very stable political structures, with very little changes in their government or lifestyle, and with high social and political and emotional security seem to have the lowest response rate," he says.

"Some countries which do not have that kind of secure situation may have a higher response rate. Examples of these are Spain, Portugal, Italy, Ireland and Finland," he continues. "We have also found that the more we share the Gospel in the particular situation, the higher the response rate. There seems to be a multiplication process involved. The more we share the Gospel with a particular target group, the more people in that group talk about their experience to each other, the result being that there is a certain expectation and positive attitude in the minds of people when we go and present the message," he says.

Still, the overall response rate to the Gospel has not changed that much in the last decade, Lehtinen thinks. "Perhaps the peak time of the Jesus Movement created more positive expectations in the minds of the younger generation," he says. "During those years, the response rate was a bit higher than it is now. But basically the average has remained at approximately the same level. . . The average is almost constant," says Lehtinen.

The Campus Crusade leader doesn't believe Europe is the world's hardest mission field. "But certainly Europe is *one* of the world's most difficult mission fields," he says. "It is not difficult in the discouraging way, but rather in the challenging way," he adds.

"The basic difficulty here," Lehtinen continues, "is a result of the Christian history of Europe. People tend to think that they have already tried Christianity and it did not work. This feeling of living in a 'Post-Christian Age' is the problem, or rather challenge, to us. We need to change the whole image of Christianity in the minds of Europeans, and show that it doesn't belong to the past, but to the present situation and the future of this continent," he says.

The condition of the church in Europe constitutes another challenge for Lehtinen. "Many of the churches have lost their mission, biblical basis, message and their vision in life," he laments. "They communicate a dead image of Christianity which contradicts everything we want to proclaim. We need to help them regain the vision, the basis and the life which would transform entire communities.''

Continues Lehtinen: ''Still another difficulty is that there are many countries in Europe where the present generation have never seen a revival. In many countries they haven't had large revivals for centuries. In southern Europe, they never even had the Reformation. Again that means our people here are lacking a mental image of a momentum. There are Christians in Europe that don't have that mental image, and we pray that God will help us to show them that it is possible to have a revival.''

The solution to challenges to witness, Kalevi Lehtinen thinks, is ''to bring the Gospel away from the churches and isolated Christian ghettos to the streets, homes, offices and factories.'' To penetrate such areas of European society, Lehtinen feels it is not enough to rely on experts and full-time workers. ''Therefore,'' he says, ''our purpose is to build, train and disciple Christians so that we can multiply everything which has been taught to us by God.''

The experts, however, should not be excluded. ''The thinkers, the politicians, musicians, artists are well heard here in Europe,'' he says. ''Some of the top athletes are idols in Europe also, and their testimonies will be heard if they are won to Jesus Christ. Mass media is also very important here. We cannot use television or radio in most countries, because they are not commercial, but socialized. But the newspapers, which are read in Europe much more widely than in the United States, have never yet been effectively used for the Gospel. It would be expensive but also effective, and we need to approach our mass media markets from that angle. Direct mailing may also be an alternative,'' says Lehtinen.

"In many countries we have religion taught in the schools,'' he continues. "Providing evangelistic materials for the teachers will guarantee that we can reach every person at least once in his life with the Gospel through the educational structure. Politically, we also have to fight for the freedom of preaching the Gospel in our European countries. This is not self-evident in every country anymore. But we believe that God is able to open the doors or keep the doors open for us so that the Great Commission will be fulfilled.''

Few Christians have the grasp of Christian advance in Europe as does Werner Burklin. He is now director of outreach ministries worldwide, for Youth for Christ (YFC), and is based in Geneva, Switzerland. Until July, 1977, he was director of YFC, Europe. He was succeeded in that post by George Brucks, who had been YFC's director in Holland.

A German, Burklin was born in China to missionary parents, serving under the China Inland Mission. He committed his life to Christ in a YFC rally held in Shanghai, under Bob Pierce and Dick Hillis. Much encouraged by Dawson Trotman, founder of the Navigators, Burklin returned to Europe in 1949, just after the Communists had taken China.

After training at the European Bible Institute, Paris, and Grace College, Winona Lake, Indiana, he became a YFC evangelist, and the organization's director in Frankfurt, Germany.

Youth for Christ had already established a presence in Europe by the time Burklin returned in 1949. In fact, some of the people who would later be leaders in American evangelicalism had come to Europe in the post-war years, under the auspices of YFC. Billy Graham launched YFC work in Britain in 1946. A YFC organization had sprung up in Germany in 1948, independent of a similar organization that already existed in the United States. The two later united. Workers in Europe in those early years included Cliff Barrows, Torrey Johnson, Paul Freed, Bob Evans and Bob Cook.

Now, Youth for Christ operates in nine European countries—Northern Ireland, England, Denmark, Holland, Germany, France, Switzerland, Spain and Portugal. Occasionally, there are evangelistic thrusts carried out behind the Iron Curtain, says Burklin.

Youth for Christ ministries vary in the countries, depending on local needs and opportunities. In Holland, for example, there are some 90 coffee-house centers spread across the nation. There are also youth camps, a half-way house, two boats, Bible study groups, drama and music groups in Holland, operated by YFC. "Then we have about 300 other YFC leaders spread across the country, who are active in some way or the other," Burklin says.

There are 30 full-time workers in England, mostly youth evangelists. In fact, two-thirds of the youth evangelists now at work in Britain are YFC staff members, says Burklin.

Germany also has 30 full-time YFC staffers. There, the work is primarily through churches. In addition to citywide youth crusades, training seminars and camps, YFC operates a double-decker bus called a "TEEmobil." In this "mobile coffeehouse," 8 to 10 youth travel across Germany constantly. The ministry was so successful, a second bus has been added.

"In France, Portugal and Spain," says Burklin, "we mainly work in camps, evangelistic thrusts on beaches, special tract distributions in high schools and in YFC groups in local churches."

"A very effective ministry," says Burklin, is being carried out in war-torn Northern Ireland. Evangelistic teams are sent to both Northern Ireland and to the south. There is a large film library and weekly rallies in many parts of the country.

Denmark is a new nation for YFC work. "Local ministers are interested in what we are trying to do for the young people, since very few young people go to church there," reports Burklin.

In Switzerland, most of the work is with international high schools. Many of them are the very plush institutions where the wealthy from all over the world send their children.

Combined YFC budgets in Europe amount to about one million dollars, all of which is raised in Europe. Additionally, YFC Europe helps support YFC work in India, Bangladesh, Argentina, and other parts of the world.

"Within the last four or five years, we have noted a tremendous difference in the response of European young people to the Gospel," says Burklin. "Whereas before, most of the young people didn't even know why Christ came into the world, now it seems that the youth are at least getting interested. The Christian young people are very interested in getting to know the Bible. The Bible is in and the church is out. All of the Bible Institutes and evangelical seminaries are bulging, and more young people are interested in missions than ever before," Burklin observes.

When it comes to the European church, Burklin, like Kalevi Lehtinen, sees a need for revival of vision. "European churches will have to become world mission-minded again," says Burklin. He notes that "very few missionaries, as compared to the United States, are moving out from Europe. Most churches are not interested in world missions, and very little is being taught along this line."

Eighty to 90 percent of those making commitments to Christ in meetings in Europe are young people under 20. There needs to be a continuing drive to reach the youth, coupled with more effective uses of radio, television and literature, Burklin believes.

"People, especially young Christians, will have to be taught a balanced life. All four areas of life, physical, mental, social and spiritual will have to be emphasized. Too long the Christian church in Europe has held its meetings in backyard churches. We have to learn that we can be Christians in the world and make an impact on all areas of life," Burklin says.

There are people who are offended at the suggestion that Europe is a mission field. But for the workers with Greater Europe Mission, there is no question. In their literature, they site secular sources, like the following:

Religion in France, as elsewhere in Western Europe, profoundly influenced the molding of the national culture from the late Roman occupation to the Renaissance. Philosophy, architecture, sculpture, painting, and music reflect the influence of Christianity. With the coming of the modern age, however, such influence was challenged by rational free inquiry in philosophy, and hence in other disciplines. By the 20th century, religion was no longer a major force in the society *(U.S. Department of State Background Notes)*.

and

Sweden is one of the four richest countries in the world, but 25 percent of the total Swedish population are in need of psychiatric treatment. Alcoholism in Sweden has risen by 424 percent in a decade *(Detroit News)*.

It took disaster in Navy Chaplain Robert P. Evans' own life to help him focus on Europe's need. In 1944, he went ashore with Allied forces in southern France. While scouting the countryside on a motorcycle, he struck a mine.

Evans was seriously injured, and recovery took a while. During that period, he spoke with people around him, using French he had learned as the child of missionary parents in Cameroun. As he talked, he discovered spiritual emptiness, and determined to establish a spiritual beachhead for Christ in Europe.

Evans and his wife returned to Europe in 1949, under the European Bible Institute Committee. In

Paris, they held classes in their home. Later, they rented classroom space in a building on the Seine's left bank. The Committee, in 1952, became the Greater Europe Mission and expanded its work.

"The European Bible Institute eventually found new quarters in Lamorlaye, France. Sister institutions were founded in Germany, Italy, Sweden, Greece, Spain and Portugal. Moorlands Bible College (England) and the Belgian Bible Institute, both established schools, became part of the GEM family in 1970 and 1971," says GEM literature.

The Mission's motto is, "Training Europeans to evangelize Greater Europe." The European Bible Institute continues its work in this area, with about 80 students. Zaire—formerly the Belgian Congo—has 15 times the number of evangelical Christians as Belgium itself, the Mission has found. GEM's Belgian Bible Institute seeks to address that country's need, and now has some 120 students. Sweden once sent more missionaries per capita than any other country. Yet now that situation no longer prevails, as the country has plunged into deep spiritual need. GEM operates the Scandinavian Bible Institute, with about 60 students. GEM also carries out training ministries in Portugal, Greece, Denmark, Ireland, Italy, Austria and Spain.

"Currently more than 250 missionaries serve Christ under GEM. They teach in the Mission's Bible institutes, engage in student witness, child and youth evangelism, camp and conference work, and mass and personal evangelism. . . Each year more than 100 college-age young people participate in Eurocorps, the Mission's program of summer ministry in Europe. Several short-term associates are sent to assist career missionaries every year, usually in clerical and maintenance ministries," GEM reports.

"This year approximately $2.2 million was sent for Europe," reports GEM Executive Director Don Brugman, in 1977. "These funds," he said, "were raised in North America through the efforts of our missionaries on furlough, new appointees, area field men and through the mail."

Like Youth for Christ, GEM has found increasing response among European youth. "In the last five or six years, they seem to be more open in a number of countries than in the past," says Brugmann. "As far as witnessing is concerned," he says, "generally the European is more closed about his religious beliefs and feel they are too personal to be discussed. Most Europeans would already consider themselves to be Christians, and therefore it is very difficult for them to understand that they have a spiritual need. Witnessing tends to be more on a long-term basis than it might be in the United States."

The most effective way foreign mission groups can work in Europe is through the training of nationals, says Brugmann. Hence, GEM's strong emphasis on its training institutes. "We believe this is first of all biblical, but secondly, in the event that Communism or some other force would cause us to leave we have made our impact upon nationals who shall be able to continue on better than we," he says.

Dr. Penrose St. Amant reflected on Europe as he

prepared to retire as president of the seminary at Ruschlikon, Switzerland. Europe's spiritual crisis, as he saw it, was related to a deep disturbance of the spirit, reaching around the world.

"There is a spiritual vacuum in Europe now," he said. "Europeans are not so much skeptics as bewildered. Many don't even consider the church as a viable alternative. There is a yawning indifference. The theologians are seen as trying to prove the indefensible," he said.

One of the signs of the problem in Europe is that the state church system is "in trouble." There are several reasons for that, thought St. Amant. "There is much disappointment with the theological faculties, which are supported by public funds. They are a bringing together of scholars, and that's the purpose. But there's not much in them related to the life of the church," he said.

"The Roman Catholic Church in Europe is in more trouble than most people realize," said St. Amant. "There is a fundamental split between the position symbolized by Pope Paul's refusal to go along with his commission on birth control and that represented by theologian Hans Küng (of Tübingen).

"The dimensions of secularism in Europe," St. Amant continued, "go beyond what I see in the United States. There is much Marxism among European youth."

Some of the blame can be placed on the universities of the Western world, St. Amant believes. "The idea is that the accumulation of knowledge and its dissemination is creative, contributing to the betterment of society," he said. But the problem in Europe, and elsewhere is that "common life is not really engaged by the intellectual. He studies it, and assumes that alone will be helpful." But clearly, it is not enough to rescue Europe.

"The idea of relativity is a powerful element in late modern thought," continued St. Amant. "The idea is still strong that one cannot penetrate beyond appearance to reality." What this means for Europe, he said, is that "you get young people believing morality is only a reflection of consciousness."

St. Amant noted that "Camus and Sartre [French existentialists] are immensely powerful influences in European thought now, Camus more than Sartre. Camus presents a kind of alternative to traditional heroes, to the church and to Jesus. Camus didn't really believe there was a viable basis for human dignity, but he believed in it anyway and tried to contribute to it. He refused to accept as a conclusion the idea that life is fundamentally absurd. His understanding of Christianity was through what he saw as a bigoted Roman Catholicism. Had he begun differently, it might have been an entirely different story."

J. D. Hughey has spent years observing Europe, as area secretary for Europe, the Middle East and South Asia, for the Foreign Mission Board of the Southern Baptist Convention. He believes Europe must be reached for Christ.

"Everywhere in Europe beautiful cathedrals, magnificent works of art, lovely music, and great literature remind us of our Christian origins," he says.

"The laws of most European nations and of those made up of former Europeans (like the United States) reflect Christian concepts and customs."

But Europe cannot be classified as a Christian continent, he thinks. "Several years ago a European Baptist leader said, 'Eastern Europe is officially atheistic, and western Europe is unofficially irreligious,'" recalls Hughey.

"No one should conclude that Christianity is dead in Europe," he continues. "There are many faithful believers in Christ. The Roman Catholic Church, the old Protestant state churches, and the Eastern Orthodox churches have lost numbers and power but still have quite a bit of theological and spiritual vitality." Additionally, the free churches "still play an important role. Pentecostals have demonstrated a remarkable capacity for expansion.

"Baptists and other believing Christians in Europe know they have a great missionary responsibility," he says. "Their continent, so long regarded as the center of Christendom, has become a mission field. This generation of Europeans must be evangelized."

What American Christians must do, thinks Hughey, is to "stand beside and cooperate with our Christian brothers and sisters in Europe as they try to make the attractiveness and the power of Christ known to their neighbors. . . . Perhaps a nation or a continent in our present human situation cannot become Christian. But what a difference Christians make in the places where they live!"[1]

CHAPTER SIX

Europe Beyond the Crossroads

Where will Europe go as she moves beyond the crossroads? The question is crucial for West and East. To try to find the answer, we narrowed the focus to a few basic questions. The answers hint at direction.

1. *Is Europe really moving away from its postwar humanism, materialism, existentialism and growing hungry for the Gospel?*

Kalevi Lehtinen: "I don't see much evidence that Europe would be moving away from humanism, materialism and existentialism. Perhaps there is a movement away from philosophical existentialism, but it is toward materialism or some other existentialist or mystical type, rather than towards Christianity. But at the same time, those who base their lives upon humanism and materialism seem growingly disillusioned and unhappy.

"Today, the fight in Europe is not so much be-

tween materialism and Christianity in the minds of
most people. Rather it is a struggle between one form
of materialism and another form of it, between
capitalism and Communism. But in any social or economic system, it seems that the material wealth
seems to be the highest goal of the great majority of
Europeans. The basic selfishness of people remains
the same independent of the economic system.

"We talk much about the cults and dangers of
philosophies here in Europe today. Yet I believe that
at least 90 percent of our problem is simply practical
materialism. . ."

*Henry J. Heijermans, General Director, Worldwide
European Fellowship:* "I cannot really say that
Europe is moving away from the philosophies. . .
There are individuals here and there who are ripe for
Christian ministry, but I don't believe that is true on a
national basis. A ripeness for Christian ministry is
related closely to the conviction of sin brought about
by the Holy Spirit. It seems to me this element is
greatly lacking. People here and there may be disillusioned with prosperity and all it has brought them,
but they are not ready to turn to Christ unless they
recognize sin and its consequences. We in WEF are
praying for that kind of movement."

Werner Bruklin: "There is no doubt that many
people, especially young people, are moving away
from the post-war 'isms.' Many people have noted
that materialism does not give them complete satisfaction, thus they are looking for spiritual values. But

it is quite difficult for them to make the jump from 'interest in the Gospel' and 'accepting the Gospel.' Tradition is still very strong, and since most of the people are somewhat rooted in some church, it is difficult to make them aware of their need for a Savior."

2. *There are predictions Europe will turn to Communism in the next decade. Will that happen? Can it be stopped? Is there a role for Christians to play in confronting Marxism in Western Europe?*

Penrose St. Amant: "Eurocommunism is different from Eastern Communism. But I think I see fear in the eyes of a lot of people. There's probably enough counterbalance through tradition and history to keep the countries from going to the Communists."

Werner Burklin: "I am afraid that a takeover by the Communists in the next decade may happen. All of the East is under their control, and several Western European countries are getting more Communist all the time. It is not clear whether Eurocommunism can be equated with Soviet Communism. It may be a new brand, and it is said that they are willing to cooperate with Western democratic forms. On the other hand, countries such as Germany have a trend away from leftist and Communist movements. No doubt, the Christian message will be able to help brake the Communist movement."

Don Brugmann: "It is very difficult to make any kind of determination as to what the Communist possibilities are. I think we can be encouraged by the way it has been stopped in some of the southern European countries at least temporarily. If it does come it will probably be in more of a socialistic form, at least during the initial years, and still give us a good bit of time for proclamation."

Henry Heijermans: "I would not be surprised if Communism would take over in the countries in southern Europe particularly. The type of socialism which has been preached and implemented in a number of Western European nations has certainly laid a good foundation. And it almost seems a gradual process in that direction. In that type of environment, the church will still stand because it is God's instrument. The church must confront Marxism by means of a positive declaration of the Gospel of Jesus Christ."

Kalevi Lehtinen: "I don't know whether or not Europe will become Communist soon or ever. Certainly, Communism is growing, especially in southern Europe. At present the Communism of the Latin countries in Europe is very nationalistic-oriented. The Communists there want to be independent from Moscow. This is true especially in Italy, Spain, Portugal and France. Yet, this was also true within the Communist parties of the Eastern European countries. But once they gained power, they became very faithful to Moscow. I don't believe we can base any hopes on the national image of the Western European Communist parties.

"There are also some splits within the Communist parties of Europe, and fights between the different interpretations of Communism. Maybe there are signs that the Communists are being divided into several different camps and disintegrating a bit. . .

"I believe that the best answer to Communism in Europe is not capitalism, but preaching the Gospel to every European—capitalist or Communist. The only hope for Europe is not in having a non-Communist or Communist political structure. The hope is only in Jesus Christ."

3. *So much of Western Christianity in the 20th century rose from European Christianity. What has happened to the church in Europe? Why is it reputed to be "dead" and "cold"?*

Henry Heijermans: "The Inquisition more than decimated the church in many Western European nations. The believers fled for their lives. Many moved to America in due time. Higher criticism, liberalism, neo-orthodoxy, two world wars and other political upheavals have all left their mark. When the church failed to preach the Word of God, it ceased being alive and a benefit and blessing to the people."

Don Brugmann: "I believe a good bit of the reason for Western Europe having a relatively dead church today relates to the fact that for a long time it was under state domination and did not have spiritual vitality. In fact, much of the Reformation was nothing more than changing of allegiances by masses of people and did not involve individual conversion. While there were some great things that happened during those days, it lacked much. Further, much of the Christianity of Europe was ritualistic rather than personal.''

Werner Burklin: "Traditionalism and institutionalism have bogged down European Christianity. Also, higher critics and all criticism towards the Bible certainly were detrimental to the growth of the Christian church. It was rationalism and not so much materialism that became the curse in Europe.''

Kalevi Lehtinen: "Historically, the decline of the European churches to a great extent started with the Enlightenment period of the 18th and 19th centuries. The Enlightenment meant a basic change in the thinking of man. It was a breakthrough of humanism. Before that time God was the center of the universe and the measure of all. There were no clear standards about good and bad in an absolute sense anymore. Everything became relative. Whatever was good for man was good, and whatever was bad for man was bad.

"This humanism penetrated the churches during last century in a very strong way. But before the churches, it penetrated the theological faculties and departments in the universities. A liberal theology was a direct result of this humanistic approach to life. The whole of liberal theology is based upon an assumption that we need to create theology without assuming God or anything supernatural. For instance, the origin, the writers and the miracles of the Bible must be explained without God, according to this liberalism.

"This liberal approach in the area of exegetics took place basically in the last century and the beginning of the 20th. Then a little later in the 1920s and 1930s, the theologians started to apply the same principles in the area of systematic theology and doctrine. The philosophical systems of neo-orthodoxy and some other theological schools simply were attempts to create a 'godless theology.' The last stage has been that of application of this theology. That means that the ethics and social implications of doctrine and church life have been affected by this humanistic thinking.

"All this development has greatly affected the churches of Europe. Also some of the traditional heresies have affected church life in Europe. For instance, sacramentalism and traditionalism in liturgies, sticking to old translations of the Bible and an unwillingness to change methods have affected the spiritual life of Europe. The state church structure has never proven to be really effective in reaching the populations of countries for Jesus Christ. But the structures are still so strong that it is difficult to replace them with new structures which will be more effective."

4. *Please assess overall the future of evangelism in Europe.*

Don Brugmann: "All in all, I think there are some positive elements. For instance, in our schools, we

89

are seeing an increased enrollment each year, which means that there is more potential of reaching the youth and training them than ever before. I don't especially believe that it is going to be more difficult than it has been. There has been more of an openness to evangelism by Europeans, and this is a good sign.''

Henry Heijermans: ''I am encouraged. It looks more difficult perhaps because there are so many people and there are so few who seek to reach them. However, God is able to use small things and do His great work. As I think of small ministries in our fields of Austria, France, Germany, Holland, Ireland, Italy, Luxembourg, Spain, Sweden and the United Kingdom, I cannot help but be encouraged. In some of these countries, churches are beginning to develop quite well. In others we are still struggling very much. I am optimistic and encouraged because it is the work of God. If it weren't for that fact, I would have quit a long time ago.''

Penrose St. Amant: ''The free church in Europe has a significant opportunity in the next 25 years, but it will have to relate the Gospel to the whole of European thought. We may be at the point of a significant breakthrough of the free church. More enthusiasm is needed in preaching.''

Kalevi Lehtinen: ''I believe that the Great Commission will be fulfilled in Europe. We may have more difficulties, but we will also have more victories. I am encouraged. Not that I would be an optimist, but I am encouraged because I want to be a realist. And our realism is based upon the fact that if God is with us, who can be against us?''

Werner Burklin: ''I am very much encouraged as to evangelism in Europe! I believe that the greatest days lie ahead. We need more national workers, who are dedicated to Christ and are convinced that the Bible is the inspired Word of God. We also need many more missionaries, not only from America, but also from Third World countries to present Christ in the regions of Europe where the Gospel has never penetrated. We have to make an all-out effort via radio, and if possible, through television, then through literature and large youth evangelistic thrusts to reach as many as possible. We have to build upon the lives of hundreds of young Bible institute and seminary students that have left the schools in recent years. We have to enlarge the vision to become worldwide, with a deep interest in seeing peoples in regions beyond reached for Christ. God is at work in Europe, and looking back to the last 25 years, I must say with all that has happened that the next 25 years are going to be better yet!''

Where then will Europe go beyond the crossroads?

Writing history before the fact is an all but impossible task. Nevertheless, some trends are evident, predictions can be made.

This study indicates there will be a revival of Christianity in Europe, perhaps soon. The hunger of European youth for something deeper, more substantial, is a sign of this. Their response to such efforts as the mass rallies described above and training programs also indicate reasons for hope.

Europe, like America, has seen the bleak desolation of the secular city. Theologians like Jürgen Moltmann, of Germany, who've tried to stir hope by pointing toward quasi-political structures like revolution, are singing lyrics too many Europeans have heard before. The longing now seems to be for something transcendent. Even Marxists, in the much-touted "dialogues" with Christians, have indicated the need for a stress on the transcendent.

But the revival may come midst suffering. Marxism will likely make serious inroads in European nations. It is altogether plausible to think we may someday see a Europe in which Portugal, Spain, Italy, France are dominated by Communists, and stare into the staunchly conservative eye of Germany, with the other nations clinging to forms of socialism. The Christians in the Marxist societies will have to pay a heavy price for their faith, as they do now. But the suffering may help spark the revival. The days ahead may indeed be days when the wheat and tares grow together in the European field.

But the revival *is* coming, for at least three reasons. First, simply because of the faithfulness of the Holy Spirit to honor the work his servants are doing with great dedication. Secondly, the revival is coming because of the emptiness Europeans are discovering in the philosophies so long cherished there. Finally, revival is coming because of the staying power of the

Christian workers. One of the untold stories of modern times is that of the great gains being made by the church in Africa. The work of missionaries for generations is just now bearing fruit in some areas. The same thing will happen in Europe. The route beyond the crossroads will be rocky and perilous. But many Europeans will follow the people with the Light.

CHAPTER SEVEN

Three Who Point the Way

Europe is not without strong internal voices, urging her down the path of life. While the external voices—the missionary voices—are important ones, there are those which sound from within Europe. Because they are European by birth or adoption, they speak her accents.

In too much of the 20th century, the voices within have been uncertain ones. They have suspected there was a right course for Europe to take at the crossroads, but it has frequently been voiced as only that—a suspicion, a possibility among others.

But now there are strong voices. Their tones are not laced with the possibility of non-truth. They speak with conviction. They know where they are going, and know where Europe should go for genuine life.

These voices are many, but can be represented in three whose tones are gaining important hearing beyond Europe. In fact, where once the uncertain sounds dotted and dashed from Europe, affecting

American theology, now the new ones speak, influencing not only their own regions, but the United States, and other parts of the world.

The voices of Jacques Ellul, Francis Schaeffer and Os Guinness speak of hope, the ground of hope and the living out of hope.

Jacques Ellul

Jacques Ellul hardly looks the part of a giant—especially a theological giant. The balding, mellow-faced man is not even a professional theologian. Ellul is a lawyer, more specifically, professor of law and history at the University of Bordeaux, in France.

Frequently described as a "social critic," Ellul is being accorded status as a theological giant by a growing number of students in Europe and abroad. When observers lament that Europe is no longer producing Calvins, Zwinglis and Luthers, the devotees of Ellul do not worry. For Europe is the vessel where Ellul's thought has germinated, and whence it has emerged in a score of books.

For Jacques Ellul *is* a social critic. But his critique is not cooked in the bubbling vat of his own subjective tastes, but in the scorching furnace of biblical criteria. If one classifies as a prophet that person who takes the Bible's perspectives, and uses them as the standard against which to measure all of reality, then Ellul is a 20th-century prophet.

Like the prophets of Israel's "golden age"—the eighth century B.C.—Ellul is not mired in an abstract world isolated from the idolatry he assaults. Though

Ellul is sharply mindful of humanity's political charades, he is a skilled practitioner of politics. Ellul was born in Bordeaux in 1912. During World War II, he fought the Nazis as a member of the French Resistance. Later, he served as mayor of Bordeaux. As a churchman, he is an active layman, a member of the Reformed Church of France.

In surveying Europe's relatively well-populated lists of theologians to attempt to decipher whose thought will have greatest impact in years ahead, Ellul seems a certain choice. Like Jürgen Moltmann, the German, Ellul seeks to illumine the dark, despairing European landscape with the torch of hope. But, unlike Moltmann, he does not use that torch to lead followers down a blind path of redemption by revolution.

If God is silent in the self-destructive acts of the bourgeoisie ("prevalent phagocytosis" Ellul calls it) "this God is also silent in the revolutionary lie of the holy quaternity, Marx-Lenin-Stalin-Mao, in the revolutionary farce of the third-world activists, in which the participating Christians betray Jesus Christ just as much, but in the reverse direction, as they do in the bourgeois magnificence."[1]

Mao's revolution in China, of course, has become the model for a great many of the world's people who see no hope beyond man and his political maneuvers, for world redemption. Especially after Richard Nixon opened the world's door to China in 1972 did the singers of praise gather there for a mass chorale. But Ellul would not join the chorus.

"If there are some today who see hope in China,"

he says, "that's because they don't really know what's happening there. We're in the same situation with respect to China that we were in with respect to Hitlerism in 1933 or Stalinism in 1950."[2] Later, in the same book, Ellul says, "The People's Republic of China is the exact oriental counterpart of Nazi Germany."[3]

But Ellul is not castigating the Marxist East as an antiphonal chant to an oratorio of praise for the West.

> We are in the strangest possible situation, in which man is living just the reverse of what, objectively, he should be living. In the most pacified and guaranteed society which has ever existed, man is living in uncertainty and growing fear. In the most scientific of societies, man is living in the irrational. In the most liberal of societies, man is living "repression," and even hyper-repression. In a society in which the means of communication are the most highly developed, man is living in a sort of phantasmagoria. In a society in which everything is done to establish relationships, man is living in solitude. . . . It would seem as though each advance nurtures its exact opposite in man's living experience.[4]

Such ideas have caused some to label Ellul as a pessimist. But that pessimism is often in the spirit of the secular reader of Ellul who does not understand the grip of the Gospel and its burning brightness on the man. "Judgments that he is a habitual pessimist derive from those whose disgruntled humanism is based on such premises as 'man is free,' 'man is good' or 'progress is inevitable,' " says Os Guinness, of Ellul, in *The Dust of Death*.[5] Also in that book, Guinness predicted rightly that the 1970s would be a time of "increasing prominence" for Ellul, though most of his books were produced long before. And Guinness notes that even Aldous Huxley predicted that Ellul's book *The Technological Society* would be regarded as one of the "most authentic documents of social criticism" in the 20th century.

To appreciate the immensity of hope the biblical revelation stirs in Ellul, one must go the depths with him in his disenchantment with the "false kingdom" man has established, apart from God. The false kingdom has led to "the age of magicians." The reliance on the "political prophet," the "miracle-working wise man," and other technicians of the 20th century, is nothing more than the revival of ancient magic.

But the false kingdom has sired the "age of scorn" as well. "What we have here," says Ellul, "is basically the attitude of a person who is not content to conquer and dominate. He must also destroy the other person inwardly, must treat him as a thing, destroy him spiritually, repudiate him. To kill him means nothing. There is no satisfaction to be had from his death unless he has first been vilified."[6]

The false kingdom rules in the age of suspicion, continues Ellul, that time when "we have learned that only the lie is true, that only the murder of one's father is consistent with one's being, that incest with one's mother is the greatest desire, that we are never disinterested, that we are incurably insane for money, whether we have it or not, for our social class, for our childhood."

The age of derision is the natural sequel to scorn
and suspicion, says Ellul. "Derision admits of no dia-
logue, no encounter. All it allows is a pointing of the
finger, before the jeering god of mobs, at the person
who protests his innocence, and who disappears
shamed, with no chance to make a reply."[7]

To this point, Ellul seems as infected with the existentialist despair of European philosophy as a Camus
or Sartre. But because he functions in the perspective
of Christ, Ellul focuses on the negative in order to
reveal the place and power of hope.

If world society has descended to the pit the Apostle Paul wrote about in Romans 1, wherein "God
gives them up," then man is not left with a God-less
nothing, but man is left with hope, the hope for the
return of the Word. Chaos and darkness ruled prior to
creation, therefore "the creation was God's act of
hope." So now chaos and darkness rule, but "the
more scarce the Word of God becomes, the greater is
hope. It eagerly latches onto the few scraps still visible, onto the whisper, of which it seems that everything in it has been said. When God is turned away,
then, in the desert of information, nothing more is
possible but hope."[8]

The "Word" Ellul refers to so often, and on which
his personal hope rests so firmly, is the object of his
quest as he probes all areas of life. His is "the simple
attitude of the believer with his Bible who through the
text he is reading is ultimately trying to discover what
is the Word of God, and what is the final meaning of
his life in the presence of this text."[9]

But this Word is no sleepy discourse on virtue and

truth. Rather, it is a "revelation . . . ever new which cannot be systematized, nor analyzed, nor relegated to a past when it was alive but now that it has taken place it is delivered into our hands to do with it what we will."[10]

The Bible, in its simple directness, then, becomes the standard for Ellul's work. "I therefore confess," says Ellul, "in this study and this research that the criterion of my thought is the biblical revelation, the content of my thought is the biblical revelation, the point of departure is supplied by the biblical revelation, the method is the dialectic in accordance with which the biblical revelation is given to us."[11]

But, again, for Ellul, this is a living Word, the dynamic outflow of the will of a dynamic Person. Jesus Christ, as the living expression of that Person, is at the center of Christian thought, not codified ideas. Christian ethics, Ellul defines in the light of this understanding, as, "the relation between the person of Jesus Christ and a person who takes him as his Savior and Lord"[12]

Ellul elaborates on Christ as center in *The Presence of the Kingdom:* "We must be convinced that there are no such things as 'Christian Principles.' There is the Person of Christ, who is the principle of everything. But if we wish to be faithful to Him, we cannot dream of reducing Christianity to a certain number of principles (though this is often done), the consequences of which can be logically deduced."[13]

It has been noted that the Christianity the existentialist, Jean Paul Sartre, was exposed to as a youth was a distorted version represented by the Roman

Catholic Church in France. Had Sartre had a more complete vision of Christianity, goes the conjecture, he might not have opted for atheism. When it comes to Ellul and the church in general, it is too easy to conclude that he is reacting in the context of the church with which he is familiar—European Protestantism, with its state churches and stagnant institutionalism. It does seem that Ellul sweeps too widely in his generalizings about the church. Understandably, he is unaware of the cleansings of renewal which have moved through some branches of the church, in his writings prior to the seasons of renewal. But there is no debate in the fact that for all the activities of the church, the world is yet unredeemed, unchanged.

"Mediocrity" is Ellul's big complaint with the church. The problem is not so much in the fact that the church is wealthy, because, as he says, "she is just as mediocre where her membership is proletarian and antibourgeois."[14]

The church in this mediocrity reminds Ellul of the Petain period in France, a time he would remember painfully, as a member of the French Resistance. The church collaborates and compromises with the world, complains Ellul. The theologians of the left tingle with excitement when they feel the Marxists have listened to something they are saying. And, Ellul could have added, churchmen of the right are just as enthused by popular acceptance of their church by their approved cultures.

The church is fractured, and Ellul has little confidence in the attempts of various groups to unite it. He says he has seen nothing in recent years to alter his conviction that organized ecumenical activities "have meant the death of ecumenism because of the crushing dominance of the bureaucratic machine."[15]

Ellul, a churchman, is by no means opposed to the idea of church as institution. But without the intervention of the Holy Spirit that institution is nothing more than a sociological body, and human mechanics within the institution stifle the spontaneity of the Holy Spirit.

Ellul also worries over the "dryness" of the church. By "dryness," he refers to a lack of witnessing, of sharing Christ's message. It is the Holy Spirit who makes people hear the Gospel, says Ellul. That is the clear teaching of the Bible. That being so, Ellul has concluded that the Holy Spirit isn't speaking anymore through the church.

Evidences of this, he says, include widespread indifference to the Gospel. But surprisingly, he notes, while the Gospel is being rejected, there is a sharp interest in religion. "The fact that man turns to religion, or to religions, at the same time that he rejects the revelation of God and of Jesus Christ is a plain indication that God remains strictly hidden,"[16] says Ellul.

But the Spirit of God has also been dismissed by human attempts to make the Bible understandable apart from the intervention of the Holy Spirit. "The passion for language analysis and hermeneutics is the unintentional expression of God's silence,"[17] Ellul says. Modern practioners of biblical interpretation, including, one assumes, those who use the historical-critical method, so crucial a tool in European theology, undertake biblical interpretation with the attitude, "We shall stay within the domain of the human. That's where the problem has to be worked out."[18]

Ellul sounds like other experts on European Christianity, who've blamed the spiritual lethargy there on the approach of the academics toward the Bible. Form criticism, he says, "is a reduction process which looks scientific, and which in this case is a process of spiritual poverty."[19]

The conformity of the church to the world is another concern of Ellul's, because he fears the church's resemblance to the world at many points indicates the absence of the "Wholly Other" who alone can make the church wholly different from worldly bodies.

Ellul has analyzed the situation vis-à-vis the world accurately. The picture is a dismal one. To him, it appears that humanity has strayed so far from God that the conditions of Romans 1 have been met, and God has abandoned mankind.

Yet, again, this is the point of greatest hope. Ellul reminds us that there has never been abandonment as severe as that experienced by Christ on the cross, when he cried, "My God, my God, why hast thou forsaken me?" Yet, later, still on the cross, Jesus would thunder, "It is finished!" and, "Father, into thy hands I commend my Spirit."

In terms of Europe's present need and the greatest potential of his impact, Ellul's hope stands out. For

Europe at the crossroads wants to find something beyond pessimism and despair. It has plowed that dismal rut too many decades. Those who would call it to hope often point to human reason. But Europe has seen that counterfeit, in the terrorism and emptiness of the French Revolution. Others would seek to light hope's flame through an appeal to technology. But that, too, is an old refrain, sung by Speer and his munitions workers as they cranked out arms for Hitler.

Nor do European "theologians of hope," like Moltmann, point the way. Ellul himself tells why, in his commentary on Revelation, *Apocalypse:* "Indeed, to conceive that history ends inevitably and normally in the Kingdom, by technical progress or by political revolutions; to conceive that God acts in history by the intermediary of the political actions of man, revolutionry or conservative, is the complete opposite of hope."[20]

Moltmann leads us to human revolutions, which sour, and grow inhumane. Ellul leads us to God. If what he says is true, if the times of "abandonment" can be preludes to the surprising intervention of God, then beneath Europe's dour, somewhat dismal countenance there rings the laughter of a joyfully anticipated future. Ellul is Europe's true "theologian of hope."

Francis Schaeffer

If Ellul is a better voice for Europe on hope, then Francis Schaeffer's is an infinitely better trumpet on biblical scholarship than Bultmann, Barth, even, and a score of European theologians who have contrived the hermeneutics Ellul so loathes.

True, Schaeffer is not a European. But anyone who's talked with Schaeffer knows that more than 30 years as a resident of Europe have molded him into as typical an Alpine dweller as can be found, from his goatee to his knickers. Besides, Schaeffer is as European as was Tillich American.

The route to Francis Schaeffer's collection of chalets high in the Swiss Alps—known as L'Abri— covers territory one assumes only exists in fantasy. The railroad track to the village of Aigle, jumping-off place for L'Abri, hugs Lake Geneva. The lake itself is punctuated with snow-topped peaks.

At Aigle, there is a bus which travels to Huemoz, higher in the Alps, where some of the chalets are located.

It is a glistening April day. Surprisingly, there are no clouds. The air thins with the altitude. It begs to be breathed. As the bus gropes higher, the deep plunges into the Rhone Valley become visible. Miniscule farms range the meadows below. They are emerald-green, spattered with golden mounds of stacked hay.

A lady snatches us from the vista, announcing that the next stop will be Huemoz. The bus stops just in front of Chalet Melezes, once the home of the Schaeffers, now one of the lodging-study centers for the students who come from all over the world inquiring about the Christian faith, looking for spiritual "shelter" (*L'Abri,* in French, means "shelter").

It is 11 in the morning. Our appointment with Schaeffer is at 3 P.M. He has just returned from the

United States, where he has been touring with his film and book, *How Should We Then Live?* Schaeffer has the flu. But true to his legendary hospitality, he insists he will see us anyway.

The students invite us to a seminar, to be held in another chalet. Only L'Abri residents are allowed to discuss in the seminars, but guests may listen. The grounds are muddy, and we remove our shoes. Fifty of us sit along the floor of the chalet. Heavy topics concerning the justice of God and His mercy lumber across the room.

At lunch, they refuse to take payment. We eat the sandwiches and soup and continue the conversations about heavy things. Then my host says, "you'll need to leave about 2 . . . it takes an hour to walk up to Chesieres."

And so it is, we find ourselves climbing an alp to see Francis Schaeffer. But we are convinced that no understanding of Europe's destiny can be had without a discussion with the man who has so thoroughly merged with Europe that he sees it through the eyes of an American transplant who thinks like a European.

Schaeffer and his family came to Europe not long after World War II for mission service. Gradually, the ministry evolved to a special concern for students and wandering youth impaled on sharp thorns of doubt and faithlessness. Schaeffer's philosophical approach to Christian apologetics communicated with them, and over the years a profound work has gone forward. Additionally, Schaeffer has written many books, all coming at Christian witness from his conservative, philosophical perspective.

For Schaeffer, the dilemma of Christian witness in Europe deals with the attitude toward the Bible cultivated in its seminaries. Many European pastors cannot raise hope and commitment and faith in their parishioners because they themselves have been taught to disbelieve or to question everything they read in the Bible. Such ministers simply have nothing to believe, thinks Schaeffer.

"The real issue is the view of the Bible the church has always held," Schaeffer tells us. "If you use that as a definition, one must be faced with the fact there are very few Bible-believing people in Europe. This is the dilemma."

The hope of the United States is in the fact that there are "more Bible-believing seminaries than in the rest of the world combined." The majority of the seminaries in Europe do not have a high enough view of the Scripture, thinks Schaeffer. This is the result of higher criticism, a method of Bible interpretation Schaeffer believes does little more than reduce the Bible to interesting literature.

"The church is constantly in danger of conforming to the thought patterns of history," he says. "Liberal theology [the brand he believes has overwhelmed the European schools] has been nothing but secular thought forms put in religious terms, several years later." Schaeffer believes the despairing existentialism of postwar Europe has died "as a philosophy." "But the methodology is still with us," he says. And that again, thinks Schaeffer, is a problem with training of ministers in Europe. They are led simply to ape their culture. "This is a period of pessimism," he says.

Consequently, Schaeffer believes the only way to save Europe now is to "build almost from the ground up." There must be a recovery of a strong view of the Bible, he believes. This view must take center stage at seminaries and theological institutes. Only then will pastors have the zeal to lead their church members to be vibrant witnesses.

One of his basic concerns is that some Eastern European countries are permitting theological students to train at some Western European seminaries. Schaeffer hopes they are not loosing from the firm Scriptural moorings which characterize evangelicalism in Eastern Europe.

Schaeffer's view of the Bible has come, largely, from decades of grappling with ideas emerging from the European universities and floating ultimately, in ponderous convoys, across the Atlantic to America.

Schaeffer meets the issues of interpreters like Bultmann head-on. Rudolph Bultmann taught that the Bible contains truth, but that truth is dressed in the pleasant garments of myth-event. To get to the truth, one must remove the myth, and see the *beyond*. Historicity is but a side issue. The important thing is to get beyond peripheries like that.

Karl Barth, of Basel, taught that that part of the Bible which is true, is objectively true.

Schaeffer takes on the extreme of Bultmann and the more moderate mistake of Barth. In a speech before the International Congress on World Evangelization, in Lausanne, Switzerland, in 1974, Schaeffer stated clearly what he believed to be the issue.

"The heart of neo-orthodox existential theology is that the Bible gives us a quarry out of which to have religious experience but that the Bible contains mistakes where it touches that which is verifiable—namely history and science," said Schaeffer.

For Bultmann and his disciples, history and science, in the contexts of the Bible, would be part of the "myth." For Barth, they might be part of the incidental. For Schaeffer, if history and science do not stand, the nature of the Bible itself does not stand.

"The issue is whether the Bible gives propositional truth (that is, truth that may be stated in propositions) where it touches history and the cosmos, and this all the way back to pre-Abrahamic history, all the way back to the first eleven chapters of Genesis, or whether instead of that it is only meaningful where it touches that which is considered religious," said Schaeffer, in the Lausanne speech.

Schaeffer recalls with distaste an apparent joke Darwin's friend, T. H. Huxley, made. In 1890, Huxley said he foresaw the day when faith would be separated from all fact, and that faith would go on triumphant forever. Schaeffer saw in this remark the sly suggestion that nothing backs up faith anyway. But he fears that those who deny the science and history of the Bible are removing the fact on which the faith rests.

Indeed, Schaeffer douses the idea of "blind faith," sometimes the pious claim of well-intending Christians. Faith in God is never blind because it is faith in One Who has performed in history. This is a point Schaeffer stresses in his commentary on Joshua.

Further, Schaeffer sees the biblical revelation as the sole alternative for society's survival, not the biblical revelation *plus* some understanding of man, or some work of man.

In light of the tragedies humanity now drowns in, "it seems that there are only two alternatives in the natural flow of events: first, imposed order or, second, our society once again affirming that base which gave freedom without chaos in the first place—God's revelation in the Bible and His revelation through Christ."[21]

The "imposed order" would be that of the technocrats, scientists, behaviorists whose mechanistic view of man permit all sorts of experimentation "in the human interest." But they are as ghastly as the control systems of a Skinner and the biological experimentation C. S. Lewis wrote about in *That Hideous Strength,* and now being carried out in laboratories around the world.

But Schaeffer warns against a biblical faith based simply on a desire to preserve human society. "Christian values, however, cannot be accepted as a superior utilitarianism, just as a means to an end. The biblical message is truth and it demands a commitment to truth,"[22] he says. Schaeffer's biblical commitment, then, is at the purest level. One commits oneself to the Scripture, not because it leads to a fulfilling lifestyle—though it does that—nor because it is expedient for society's survival—though it is

111

that—but because it is truth, and, by itself, merits such commitment.

Through such insistence on the absolute, objective truth of the totality of Scripture, Schaeffer stands in bold contrast to that bulky load of European theology which sounds an uncertain—or at best, a one-note—trumpet on the Bible. If Europe is to travel the right direction from the crossroads, it must recognize truth. Schaeffer's approach to the Bible will serve that need far better than the theological voices Europe has listened to usually in the 20th century—when it has listened at all.

Os Guinness

If Ellul speaks at the point of hope, Schaeffer at the point of the ground of hope as expressed in the Bible, then Os Guinness, a disciple and associate of Schaeffer, points the way in terms of cultural expression of biblical truth.

Obviously, the contributions of the three cannot be so easily separated. Ellul, as we've seen, has a powerful Bible-centeredness. Schaeffer, say his critics, does not speak enough of hope, but no one can hold the high view of Scripture which he does without pulsating with its hope. And so Os Guinness appeals to the Scripture, outlines the grim skeleton of human culture, and speaks of hope.

But Ellul, Schaeffer and Guinness have unique themes, which, if heard, would help Europe as it ponders the crossroads.

Guinness is a scholar, a world traveler who was

born in China and educated at the University of London. He has been a close associate of Schaeffer, without living in Schaeffer's shadow. One of the most piercing commentaries on culture written from a Christian perspective is Guinness' *Dust of Death*. It is there he speaks most directly to the need of European culture as it hovers at the crossroads.

"What is needed is nothing short of Reformation and Revival, a rediscovery of the Truth of God by his people and a renewal of the Life of God within his people,"[23] says Guinness. But, like Ellul, he distrusts human attempts to bring such about. "This is our crying need individually and corporately, but both are the prerogative of God,"[24] says Guinness.

The lines of culture are being redrawn, so that Christians now face circumstances similar to the early church, thinks Guinness. "On one side the early Christians faced the obvious threat of totalitarian Roman power, while on the other they faced the more insidious threat of gnosticism in all its amorphous, many-headed guises. . . . It was in exactly this situation that the early Christians were first recognized as 'the Third Race.' "[25]

The challenge now for Christians, as they face their cultures, live within them, is to discover what it means to travel the "Third Way." "How often," writes Guinness,

> in the contemporary discussion a sensitive modern man knows that he cannot accept either of the polarized versions offered to him! Left versus right, radical versus establishment, Marxist versus Anarchist, idealist versus pragmatist, practi-

cal revolution versus mystical revolution of consciousness, optimism with no basis versus realism veering on despair, activism versus escapism—all these are polarizations born of the loss of center, of the death of absolutes. In Christianity, however, there can be a Third Way, a true middle ground which has a basis, is never compromise and is far from silent.[26]

The Christian who travels this Third Way will become a radical in the truest sense of the word. That is, the Christian radical will not seek *"to tear up by the roots,* but *to cut through to the roots,"*[27] says Guinness. And, this will be constructive radicalism, not in accord with that part of the church which is among the world's leading reactionaries.

But, again, Guinness is speaking of a *Third Way,* a system of change not now being seriously pursued by Establishment or anti-Establishment forces in the West or East. "To prevent from being off center, the Christian radical will be a man of God and a man of God's Word. The Scripture will be his script of truth. What God says in the Bible will be both necessary and normative to him in all his thought and action. Without this, Christian radicalism will merely be the momentary avant garde, speciously modern, but eventually destructive, wielding a dangerous weapon that will rebound like a boomerang."[28]

How much more preferable is Guinness' constructive radicalism, seeking to probe humanity's roots in God, working for change, than the empty alliances of terrorism some churchmen embrace! The World Council of Churches, the Geneva-based organization, needs to meet Guinness. For that body has been helping support terrorist groups, and seems, at times, almost unaware of the possibility of God's intervention in human crisis.

In the face of the young European idolizing the grand assaults of the anarchists, Guinness does not wave a white flag, and invite them to join him in holding it. He waves at them the banner of challenge. For Guinness, Christian radicalism is a challenge to compassion in a world of cold political maneuverings. It is the challenge of true understanding. The compassion of the Christian radical will feel the outrage against evil Jesus felt when He saw the creation of God shattered by Satan's works of destruction. The Christian radical will note the life of Jesus, and himself learn the reality of identification.

But Guinness does not present another brand of elitism. His is no world of exclusive entrances, with restrictive signs on the doors. "The Third Race is not a super race, not a master race, an elite of the wise, the strong and the bold."[29] The Third Race is born of God, in whose image all people are made, and before whom all people are significant.

By stressing such themes, Guinness joins with Ellul, Schaeffer, and hundreds of other voices, showing clearly that Europe is not the spiritual desert it might think itself to be, nor the angry wilderness some American Christians suspect it to be. Its spiritual terrain may be rocky, thorn-laden and rugged. But it is not barren.

NOTES

Chapter Two

[1]*Time Magazine*, June 20, 1977, p. 49.
[2]*New York Times*, July 17, 1976.
[3]*Ibid.*
[4]Will Durant, *The Story of Civilization: The Age of Faith* (New York: Simon and Schuster, 1935), p. 73.
[5]Lane Dennis, *A Reason for Hope* (Old Tappan, New Jersey: Revell, 1976), pp. 91, 92.
[6]*Op. cit.*, p. 864.
[7]W. K. Ferguson and G. Brunn, *A Survey of European Civilization* (4th ed.; Boston: Houghton Mifflin, 1934), p. 241.
[8]*Op. cit.*, p. 58.
[9]*Ibid.*, p. 60.
[10]*Op. cit.*, p. 103.
[11]*Ibid.*, p. 122.

Chapter Three

[1]*Time Magazine*, September 12, 1977, p. 29.
[2]*Ibid.*
[3]*The National Review*, September 16, 1977, p. 1051.

Chapter Four

[1]*The Commission*, June, 1977, pp. 2-6.
[2]*Ibid.*
[3]*Diakona*, Vol. II, No. 1, 1976.
[4]Use of the word "believers" in this context does not necessarily refer only to Christians: It refers to all those who accept theistic tenets, as opposed to those who accept atheistic tenets.

Chapter Five

[1]*The Commission*, August, 1977.

Chapter Seven

[1]Jacques Ellul, *Hope in Time of Abandonment*, trans. C. Edward Hopkin (New York: Seabury, 1973), p. 263.
[2]*Ibid.*, p. 20.
[3]*Ibid.*, p. 56.
[4]*Ibid.*, p. 8.

[5]Os Guinness, *The Dust of Death* (Downers Grove, Illinois: InterVarsity, 1973), p. 131.

[6]Ellul, *Hope in Time of Abandonment*, p. 43.

[7]*Ibid.*, p. 55.

[8]*Ibid.*, p. 222.

[9]Jacques Ellul, *The Politics of God and the Politics of Man,* trans. Geoffrey Bromiley (Grand Rapids: Eerdmans, 1972), p. 12, note 2.

[10]Jacques Ellul, *To Will and to Do,* trans. C. Edward Hopkin (Philadelphia: Pilgrim Press, 1969), p. 204.

[11]*Ibid.*, p. 1.

[12]*Ibid.*, p. 88.

[13]Jacques Ellul, *The Presence of the Kingdom,* trans. Olive Wyon (New York: Seabury, 1967), p. 52.

[14]Ellul, *Hope in Time of Abandonment*, p. 132.

[15]*Ibid.*, p. 137.

[16]*Ibid.*, p. 140.

[17]*Ibid.*, p. 141.

[18]*Ibid.*

[19]*Ibid.*, p. 142.

[20]Jacques Ellul, *Apocalypse: The Book of Revelation,* trans. George W. Schreiner (New York: Seabury, 1977), p. 62.

[21]Francis Schaeffer, *How Should We Then Live?* (Old Tappan, New Jersey: Revell, 1976) p. 252.

[22]*Ibid.*

[23]Guinness, *The Dust of Death*, p. 367.

[24]*Ibid.*

[25]*Ibid.*, p. 368.

[26]*Ibid.*, p. 369.

[27]*Ibid.*, p. 373.

[28]*Ibid.*, p. 375.

[29]*Ibid.*, p. 390.